HAVING
THE MIND
OF CHRIST

A study in Philippians
by
Roy W Taylor

Taken from sermons preached over many years.

First published in April 2019.

Thanks to Michelle McCabe for producing this fine cover and to Elaine Amy Orr McFeeters for checking the proof.

Published by Roy Taylor

CONTENTS

Introduction 5

Chapter 1   The People Involved 6

Chapter 2   Thanksgiving for New Converts 11

Chapter 3   Something Shared 16

Chapter 4   Prayer for Growth 20

Chapter 5   Negative Situation – Positive Results 24

Chapter 6   Preaching the Gospel 28

Chapter 7   A Good Outcome 32

Chapter 8   Of Life and Death 36

Chapter 9   Living Lives Worthy of the Gospel 40

Chapter 10   Some Christian Qualities 45

Chapter 11   How We Relate to Others 49

Chapter 12   The Incarnation of Jesus 53

Chapter 13   The Ministry of Jesus 57

Chapter 14   The Exaltation of Jesus 61

Chapter 15   A Healthy Fellowship 65

Chapter 16   Lights in the Darkness 69

Chapter 17   The Effect on Paul 73

Chapter 18   About Timothy 77

Chapter 19   About Epaphroditus 81

Chapter 20   External and True Religion 85

Chapter 21   A Change of Attitude 89

Chapter 22   What has Changed?.................................... 92

Chapter 23   Paul's Goals 95

Chapter 24   Paul's Progress 99

Chapter 25   Christian Maturity 103

Chapter 26   Two Kinds of Future 106

Chapter 27   Questions of Relationship 110

Chapter 28   The Most Important Relationship 113

Chapter 29   Food for the Mind.................................... 116

Chapter 30   The Secret of Contentment 120

Chapter 31   Christian Giving 124

Chapter 32   Final Greetings... 128

INTRODUCTION

I am an ordinary human being with all the foibles, limitations, weaknesses and failures that beset other human beings. The only difference is that I have put my trust in Jesus Christ. Now that I call myself a Christian I have a different outlook on life from that of the non-Christian. Speaking of himself and of other Christians, Paul declares that 'we have the mind of Christ'.

So often it does not feel like that. We are so aware of our human limitations. When we look at the character of Jesus, everything is so perfect, and we, by contrast, seem a long way from that.

We are aware too of how different we are from one another. Each of us has his or her own abilities, preferences, character and so on. We therefore express ourselves in different ways; yet it is the mind of Christ that governs us despite all these differences. We are not clones but we are committed to Jesus and his guidance.

What does it mean in practice that Paul, when writing to the Philippians, can say that we have the mind of Christ? That is the subject we are going to explore as we examine this letter in depth.

This book depends a lot on sermons I have preached over many years based on the epistle. It could be described as the most practical part of Paul's writings.

I write not as an expert but as one who, like all other Christians, is still in a process of learning, despite my many years and long experience. I hope I shall also have the mind of Christ as I attempt to put these thoughts together.

Chapter 1
THE PEOPLE INVOLVED
(1:1-2)

It is interesting to observe how much good Christian writing has come out of prisons. When Bunyan wrote 'Pilgrim's Progress', which some people place as second only to the Bible, he was in prison. Some of Bonhoeffer's most moving statements come from his book, "Letters and Papers from Prison". In the same way, Paul wrote some of his most important letters about the faith while he was in prison. Such is the context of the letter which we are studying here.

When we look at Paul's letters, they usually begin with three introductory features. These are the writer, the recipients and a form of greeting.

(1) The Writer

This letter purports to be not from Paul alone, but also from Timothy. It was a time when Paul was imprisoned for his faith, probably in Rome. Although Timothy appears to have been with him at the time, this does not mean that he was also a prisoner, for Paul promises to send Timothy to them. It is appropriate, however, to mention the name of this young man because, when Paul founded the Church at Philippi, as we find recorded in Acts 16, Timothy was with him. Local Christians would therefore look to both of these men with great respect. There is no indication, however, that Timothy took part in the actual writing of this letter.

I find it a great privilege to have contact still with people whom, by the Lord's grace, I have in the past been able to help in some way on the road to faith. Two of those with whom I am still in contact I first knew in my early twenties when I was running a children's club at my home church in Blackpool.

Paul could have boasted about his role as an apostle. He had led so many people to Christ. Yet he uses a very different word here to describe himself. He calls Timothy and himself 'servants of Jesus Christ'. The word may also be translated as 'slaves'. When you are leading others in the Church, you spend a lot of time standing in front of others, sharing messages from God. It would be only too easy in such circumstances to grow proud because of the status this gives. (I once had a lay reader who suffered such a doubtful reputation.) But there is no pride in Paul's description of himself. He is content to be a slave.

But he is not any sort of slave. He is a slave of Jesus Christ. That is, he has the greatest master of all. In a noble household, the glory would go to the master, not to the slave, yet in a sense it was a privilege for a slave to work for a noble master. Paul regards himself as greatly privileged since his own master is none other that Jesus himself.

Those of us who are called to Christian leadership must never forget the nature of this relationship. In the late Victorian era, one Bishop Riddings of Southwell produced a liturgy for the clergy. One part of it reads: "From self-conceit and vanity and boasting, from delight in supposed success and superiority, raise us to the modesty and humility of true sense and taste and reality; and from all the harms and hindrances of offensive manners and self assertion, save us and help us, we humbly beseech Thee, O Lord."

(2) The Recipients

Now we take a look at the recipients of this letter. He is writing to Christians who live in Philippi. These he calls 'saints', 'God's people' or 'God's holy people', depending which translation you are using. Sometimes we think of 'saints' as people portrayed in stained glass or icons; but here he is speaking of real, living people. A saint is someone who is called out from the rest of the people to belong in a special way to God. We can look at this in a negative and a positive sense.

Negatively, we are called to be separate from sin. It does not mean that a Christian never sins, for, sadly, none of us is perfect. But it means we do not persist in the same blatant sins. We seek God's help to choose rightly when temptations come upon us. It does not mean either that we never associate with sinners. To do that we would have to go and live on a desert island. But it means that, though living among sinners, we do not share their outlook. As we read in Psalm 1:1: "Blessed is the one who does not walk in step with the wicked or stand in the way that sinners take or sit in the company of mockers". I also like the J. B. Phillips translation of Romans 12:2: "Do not let the world squeeze you into its own mould".

Positively we are separated unto God. The two ideas come together in Romans 6:11: "In the same way, count yourselves dead to sin but alive to God in Christ Jesus". Sometimes people think of Christians as negative: they don't do this, don't do that. But living for God is a very positive thing. At work you may have a boss whom you really admire, and so you do your best to please him in the way you go about your work. But in our relationship with God in Christ the standard is so much higher; so we read in 1 Corinthians 5:15: "And he died for all, that those who live should no longer live for themselves but for him who died for them and was raised again".

There are two other causes for encouragement here. First of all, Paul is writing to *all* the saints. He has not just chosen Lydia or others of special consequence. All those who have trusted in Christ may be called saints.

The second encouragement is found in their relationship with Jesus Christ. They are not trying hard to live good lives without any outside help. They are already in a special relationship with Jesus Christ, and that is what enables them to live as saints.

Paul is not just speaking here to the saints in general, but in particular to the overseers and deacons. Although in a sense all Christians are equal, there are some who have been given the responsibility of providing leadership over the others. These are particularly in need of God's help so that they may fulfil that role properly. The 'overseer' is something like today's 'bishop', but without all the trimmings. The deacon's work would be more administrative. God needs people of different abilities and with different responsibilities to carry out his work and to provide much needed leadership. It has been my privilege to spend so much of my life in such spiritual service.

(3) The Greeting

After stating from whom the letter came and to whom it was addressed, Paul brought greetings to the recipients. The words used here are to be found often in his letters. They are 'grace' and 'peace'.

The simple definition of 'grace' is 'undeserved favour'. We are called Christians not because we have worked hard to gain sufficient good points. When I was working hard for a BA degree at university, I was conscious that I must earn this distinction simply by my hard work. But we cannot earn God's favour through hard work. We are told in Ephesians 2: 8: "For it is by grace you have been saved, through faith - and that is not from yourselves, it is the gift of God". This is still so. God gives us salvation as a gift, for we shall never be good enough to earn it. If we fall into serious sin, we do not have to start all over again: we must deeply repent, claim forgiveness and learn once again to enjoy God's magnificent gift. As we go on in the Christian life, we hopefully learn more and more about enjoying God's presence, but this is still not a case of earning through merit but of accepting God's grace.

The other word is 'peace'. It is a relationship: we are no longer God's enemies but we are at peace with him. Peace is a condition, but it leads to a feeling: because of what he has done for us we now feel close to God. We are no longer his enemies, for he does not hold our sin against us. We know that we belong to him, and this gives us a wonderful feeling of peace. If we lose that sense of peace, it is often because of sin. This means we must confess our wrongdoing as soon as we become aware of it, that God's peace may once again dwell in our hearts.

These gifts of grace and peace come to us from God our Father. Those of us who are parents desire the best for our children. So God our Father desires the best for us. He does it by linking us with his Son, Jesus Christ. Only Jesus can call him Father through natural affinity; when we call God our Father it is because through Christ we have been adopted as sons and daughters.

If there is so much to learn from a mere greeting, then there are many precious truths that await us as we look at the main body of this letter.

Are you experiencing grace and peace in your own life?

Chapter 2
THANKSGIVING FOR NEW CONVERTS
(1:3-6)

At the gym which I attend there is a steam room. After a period of strenuous exercise, it is good to sit there and refresh those tired muscles. In the early days of my membership I used to see a Christian man who belonged to a very successful church in Belfast. "Three more people saved last Sunday," he would declare with great satisfaction, and I would try to recollect when was the last time we had seen a new convert in churches where I was serving during my so-called retirement.

The sad thing is that there are so many churches where an individual conversion is a rare event. We read stories of multiple conversions overseas and we hear of lively London churches full of new converts such as Holy Trinity, Brompton, where Alpha courses originated, but for many of us in the local situation conversion is the exception rather than the rule.

Paul was at work in the early days of the Christian faith. He saw himself as an evangelist, taking the gospel to new places, and seeing people converted to Christ from a completely non-Christian background. The Philippians fell into this category, so here he gives heartfelt thanks for the new converts he has seen.

(1) Thanksgiving

First of all, he gives thanks for them every time he remembers them. He could have taken pride in his own ability to lead people to Christ. It would be only to easy for a man with a successful batch of converts to pat himself on the back. Paul, however, does not take pride in his own ability. Instead he gives thanks to God, for, although he has been the actual mouthpiece, through whose words they were converted, it was really God who changed them.

It would be only too easy also as an evangelist to move on from these new converts and to give his attention immediately to the unconverted to whom he will preach next. Whilst it is good to have an ongoing passion for souls, there is also a place for thanksgiving because of what God has already done in the lives of new converts.

When I was a missionary in Taiwan many years ago, it was my privilege to work amongst students. I did not see great numbers converted, but I am thankful to God for those few whose lives were changed. It has been my privilege in recent years to visit one of them who is a pastor in the USA and another who at the time was co-leading a house church in New Zealand. It was a great joy to me not only to see them converted but to observe God's continued work in their lives, and I still thank God for them. Our past experiences had forged an important bond between us.

(2) Joy

Paul goes on to say that he prays for them with joy. It would have been all too easy to dismiss them from his mind and to go on to bring others to conversion. However, although Paul has moved on to other places to work, he has kept these converts in his heart. It has been his privilege to lead them to Christ, but it is also his responsibility to keep them in his prayers, so that they may grow in their Christian lives; and this is not a mere chore, but a source of joy to him.

We are not told whether Paul prayed for all the individuals by name or simply prayed for the local church community as a whole. In constant travels and with many new converts being formed, it would have been hard for him to recall every single name. There would also have been converts whose names he did not know. However, we are not evangelists in the same sense, and it is much easier for us to pray for individual converts.

But Paul does not pray for them merely as a matter of course: he prays for them with joy. He rejoices at their conversion; but he also rejoices at their progress in the faith. He rejoices too in the power of

God, which has made all this possible. Not all our praying is done with joy. Sometimes we carry heavy burdens, and our prayers may include groaning. I recall a man who sometimes visited our home in Taiwan, and he prayed in this manner, as was clearly detectable for we could hear him from quite a distance! In this instance, however, observing what God has done in the lives of these new converts, Paul prays with joy.

(3) Partnership

Thirdly, he shows why he prays with joy. The words he uses here are "because of your partnership in the gospel from the first day until now". Yes, he was joyful when he thought of their conversion, but that was only the beginning of the story. They had become partners with him in communicating the Gospel. Did this mean that they prayed for Paul's work and even contributed to his support? No doubt it included this, but the primary meaning would appear to be that they were also taking every opportunity to make the Gospel known to their own friends and acquaintances.

It is good that we offer prayer and support to clergy, evangelists and missionaries, who take the good news of Jesus to others, but this must not be taken as a substitute for our own outreach. Each of us has a duty to make the Gospel known to others. If Jesus means so much to us, how can we forbear to share this with others? There is a circle of acquaintances belonging to us alone, and this gives us a great opportunity for sharing our faith.

In our work of evangelism, it gives us much encouragement when, as a result of our witness, someone puts his trust in Christ; but if that person then goes out zealously to share his faith with others, this gives us even more cause for rejoicing.

Indeed, there is a zeal in the life of a new convert which may even challenge us about the level of our own commitment.

(4) Confidence

Fourthly, he has confidence concerning them. It does not say he has confidence *in* them, but rather that he has confidence *concerning* them. His confidence lies in God, for it is God who is working in their lives to bring about these changes. The words he uses are "being confident of this, that he who began a good work in you will carry it on to completion until the day of Jesus Christ".

Since they had been converted through Paul's witness, he could have felt proud through observing their progress; but when he acknowledges that what has been achieved in them is from God, then all the glory goes to God and not to Paul.

God does not start a work and then grow tired of it. In Psalm 138 we read: "The Lord will fulfil his purpose for me".

What God has begun he will continue.

Here is a brief summary of what God does in our hearts.

First he regenerates us: that is, he gives us a whole new life which can be compared to being born all over again. Spiritual matters, which we barely understood before, now become real and special to us.

Secondly, he justifies us: he gives us the assurance that we are no longer under judgment but that he now accepts us just as if we had never sinned.

Thirdly he sanctifies us: it is not just a matter of being called righteous, but we now have the desire and the ability to put this into practice in our daily lives.

Fourthly he glorifies us: because we are now so special to him, we have the assurance that he will bring us into the glory of heaven one day, and that we shall live our present lives in anticipation of this.

Since we are fickle human beings, we sometimes start a project and then grow tired of it. Maybe in our travels we have come across a 'folly' – a building which somebody started but which, in due course, owing to lack of money or lack of enthusiasm, he abandoned when it was still not completed. But when God is truly working in our lives, we do not become a 'folly' for the work is ongoing.

Paul sees the Philippians at the early stage of their walk with God, but he believes that, since God has begun his work in them, he will continue it.

There are people who claim to belong to God. As a result of this they attend worship services, and their lives seem to reflect this; but after a while things begin to change: they are no longer very enthusiastic about worship, and their lives no longer reflect their supposed beliefs. When something new comes into our lives that is only based on our own thinking and our own resolves, there is no guarantee that it will last. Only when a work is truly from God is it going to last.

Paul here looks at the lives of these Philippians, and concludes that he can see a genuine work of God in them. That is why he is so confident in praying for them.

Does our spiritual life come from God or is it simply our own idea?

Chapter 3
SOMETHING SHARED
(1:7,8)

When we bring someone to Christ, that is not the end of the story: it is just the beginning. It is our privilege and our duty to work alongside such people and to encourage them to grow in their faith. For this reason, it is a great joy to me still to be in contact with those two friends recently mentioned who, as students, accepted Jesus as Saviour in Taiwan so long ago.

Paul was responsible for bringing many to faith. There were whole churches that he had founded. As I have suggested, it would be hard for him to recall the names of all converts; but he certainly has a concern for each new church community and its members. When he moves on to another place to preach to others, he does not lose his burden for those already converted elsewhere, but still has them in his heart.

It is such concern for them which prompted him to write this letter in the first place. In this short section he describes how important to him is this relationship that has been established.

In particular, he writes here of three things.

(1) His Heart

First he has them in his heart. It would have been all too easy for Paul to see these new converts simply as a statistic, confirming the success of his gospel ministry. But to Paul it is not statistics but people who count. It is not a matter of counting numbers, but of showing a deep concern for all individuals.

To say that he has them in his heart means that he loves and cares for them. This leads him, then, to pray for them, that God will continue the work in their hearts that he has begun. In fact, Paul has already expressed his concern that God will bring to completion the work which he has already begun in them.

In the Old Testament we read how the high priest would wear on his shoulders two stones bearing the names of the twelve tribes of Israel, (Exodus 28:11,12) for he was given a responsibility for all of them. For Paul, however, it goes deeper, for he has these people in his heart. That is, he continues to have a deep love and concern for them.

(2) His Experience of Grace

Secondly, he shares with them an experience of God's grace. Both Paul and his converts enjoy God grace in their lives. They know they enjoy his favour, despite their shortcomings. God's grace means that he looks upon us with warm acceptance whether we are worthy of it or not. This does not mean, however, that our circumstances are always favourable. Paul speaks of times when he is in chains because of his Christian ministry as well as those times when he is able to defend openly the Gospel to which he is committed in the face of opposition.

Yes, it is easy to know God is with us when things are going well; but if we are suffering for our faith this is more of a challenge. Is God really with us? Or has he abandoned us to our fate?

Such is Paul's faith that he is aware at such times that God is still with him. Whether he is imprisoned, or whether he is fulfilling his mission to evangelise, he still experiences the grace of God upon him. In addition to that, he is also aware that these Christian converts are standing alongside him through their prayers in these difficult times. Maybe some of them are also suffering for their faith, just as Paul is suffering.

If Paul had been suffering because of his own mistakes, it would have been a very different situation. But he is suffering because of faithfully doing God's work, and this can become a very positive experience.

In my own ministry I have never been put in jail. There have been times, however, when others, even church members, have opposed me because they did not agree with the way I was doing God's work, and life would have been very difficult for me had I not been conscious of the grace of God in my own life. I was a human being, weak and not exempt from making wrong decisions; but I was also conscious that friends were praying for me, and this also gave me strength.

There was another period when I was out of a job. As the Anglican Church was going through financial problems at the time, it was not easy for any one to give me a paid job. Months of waiting ensued. However, I joined a group of fellow Christians who were also having problems; and as we shared these problems together we found encouragement. Problems can have a positive effect!

I am sure that Paul, when he was suffering persecution, knew that these Christian converts were praying for him, and this must have given him strength to carry on. That was what it meant for them to share together in the grace of God.

(3) His Longing for Them

Thirdly, he shares Christ's longing for them. Sometimes when we are going through hard times, we need to know that someone cares for us. The most wonderful thing to know is that God in Christ cares for us. On occasions, however, it is hard to feel this; so God shows his care through the love of individuals who know and love us. The giving and receiving of loving care amongst Christians is a demonstration of God's love working out in practice. There are many indications in the Gospels of the way in which Jesus cares for people and yearns for them. At one time he stood on the hillside above Jerusalem and expressed his yearning for its inhabitants as a hen might yearn for its chicks. In this case, his concern was for people who did not follow him. He had a deep compassion too for the rich young ruler, even though that man chose in the end not to live as his disciple. How much do we share Christ's compassion towards the myriads around us who have chosen not to follow Christ or to whom such a concept is completely foreign? How concerned are we also for people around the world who have never heard the good news of salvation? When we read missionary biographies, we see that it is often such a deep concern which has prompted men and women to leave the comfort of their own land and to go to foreign places.

We are meant to share Christ's longing for the lost; but we are also to share his yearning for our fellow Christians. We know ourselves that it is not easy to live a good and faithful Christian life. Others around us have the same problem. If we desire the best for them, it will show in the way we pray for them and the way we treat them. It is possible to pray for others simply by name. Maybe we have prayer lists so that we do not forget to pray for them. But they are more than names on a list: they are real people with real problems, and our hearts go out to them. We do this not because we are superior in any way: some of their struggles we also experience in our own lives. Indeed, because of this we are better able to appreciate what they are going through. When we yearn for others and pray for them, we are in fact demonstrating that love and concern which Jesus already shows for us and for them. We have become his agents in this task.

How deep is our concern for our fellow Christians?

Chapter 4
PRAYER FOR GROWTH
(1:9-11)

As we have seen, Paul did not only lead others to Christ, but he was concerned for their ongoing lives. Because of this, he prayed for them.

Sometimes, when we pray for others, we are aware of specific needs – success in a job application, the conversion of a spouse, financial provision and so on. At other times we may not have access to such information, but we can still pray for their spiritual needs, which are ongoing.

Here, in praying for the Philippians, he shows concern for their greatest spiritual need; then he goes on to pray about the effects that will follow.

(1) Their Greatest Need

The need spoken of in verse 9 is that of <u>love</u>. This can be a very wide term. Indeed, the Bible distinguishes various kinds of love. There is brotherly love, love between parent and child, love between friends and erotic love; but here he writes of that special love which exists among Christians and which is the result of God's love for us. The chapter that deals most clearly with this is 1 Corinthians 13. In vv. 4-7 he writes: "Love is patient, love is kind. It does not envy, it does not boast, it is not proud. It does not dishonour others, it is not self-seeking, it is not easily angered, it keeps no record of wrongs. Love does not delight in evil but rejoices with the truth. It always protects, always trusts, always hopes, always perseveres." It is a type of love not known to the world outside. He does not mention who is the object of such love, but it is obvious that this is the love for God and for fellow Christians just mentioned.

Paul sees this not as a static love, but as something capable of growth. He prays that it may abound more and more. However much we love God and love others, there is still plenty of room for this to get better.

He goes on to mention two respects in which this love should grow. The first of these is in knowledge. When I got married, I thought I knew my wife; but our relationship grew and developed over the years that followed. When we first come to know God in a personal way also, that is not the end of the story but just the beginning: we then spend the rest of our life getting to know him better. The more fully we know God, the better we relate to one another.

I can recall a Christmas service in our little chapel in Taiwan many years ago. Suddenly, in the middle of it, we felt overwhelmed with the love of God, and this gave us a deep love for one another. This was not an experience easily forgotten. It was not something that we had planned, but it was simply God's intervention. Even after all these decades I still delight in the memory of that day. However, Paul speaks not just of a one-off experience, but of our ongoing knowledge both of God and of our Christian brethren. God wants to be active in all our thoughts and deeds.

As we come to know one another better, there is also a growth in depth of insight. The more we love God and our fellow Christians, the more capable we are of making good moral decisions. It is only too easy for us as Christians simply to go on following accepted patterns when making decisions; but God wants us, through our love, to discern what should be done in each particular situation and then to have the discernment to act upon this.

So Paul prays that Christian love may lead us to better knowledge and insight. Love is not just a feeling in the head, but something which determines our actions.

(2) The Effects of This

Paul goes on to describe various effects that derive from such love, knowledge and insight. First of all he speaks of discerning what is best. All through our lives we are faced with choices. We have to decide what is the best thing to do. We can look at this on a personal level. If we love God and we love others, it will affect our moral choices. We seek to do what is best for others, rather than simply trying to give ourselves more comfortable lives.

We can also understand this on a wider level. What is an individual church trying to do? Attract more people to the services through modern music? Build a more attractive auditorium? Make a bigger impact on the community as a whole? Surely it is important that we are so filled with love for God and for one another that our church will be a community that draws others in simply because of the way its members behave. It is this love also which enables church members, especially the leaders, to live consistent lives and to make good and wise decisions that will have a positive effect both on church and community.

Secondly, he speaks of being pure and blameless. Let us think of the use of a sieve. As we shake it, the pure substance remains in the sieve, and extraneous matter falls through the holes. There are things in our lives which need to be repudiated so that what remains is pure and good.

The expression used here may also refer to pure sunlight. Maybe I am buying something from a shop, but in the darkened interior it is not easy to see that purchase clearly. Only as I take it out into the sunlight can I see it properly. God wants our lives to be such that the shafts of sunlight reveal their purity.

It is possible to seem pure and blameless to others, even when there are hidden faults; but God knows us intimately, and if there are impurities within us he is aware of them. He wants to deal with us in such a way that our lives may honour him.

A day is coming when our true nature will be revealed. It is 'the day of Jesus Christ' – the time when he will return to collect those who are his. If we are indeed pure and blameless, then that will be made clear on that day.

Thirdly we are to be 'filled with the fruit of righteousness'.

Not far from where I live there used to be a fruit farm. We could go there and pick as many strawberries, raspberries and other fruit as we liked, provided that we paid for these before leaving. It was good to go there in the height of the season, when the fruit was abundant, and we could come away with ample supplies. Sadly, that site is no longer functioning. All I can do is walk down the road to a place where blackberries are growing and pick these, with the bonus that they do not cost me anything – except my labour. These I store in the freezer and pull out in order to prepare special desserts for my guests.

We are to be like those fruit bushes, producing lots of good fruit. This is how Paul puts it in Galatians 5:22-3: "But the fruit of the Spirit is love, joy, peace, forbearance, kindness, goodness, faithfulness, gentleness and self control". He is not saying here that one Christian demonstrates joy, another forbearance and so on. The ideal is that every Christian produces the whole array of fruit.

In the present verse, however, only one kind of fruit is mentioned – the 'fruit of righteousness'. Because Jesus died for us, the just for the unjust, we can be forgiven and called righteous; and through the gift of the Spirit we are empowered to live righteous lives. If we live such a life, we should incorporate all those fruits which have just been described. It is interesting to note also that love tops Christian virtues.

On this matter of 'fruit', Matthew 7:18 reads: "A good tree cannot bear bad fruit, and a bad tree cannot bear good fruit." It is the fruit that reveals who a person really is.

If we are living such a life, it is not so that we may receive the plaudits of men. Verse 11 of this chapter says that all this is 'to the glory and praise of God'.

Does God's love for me have practical effects in my own life?

Chapter 5
NEGATIVE SITUATION –
POSITIVE RESULTS
(1:12-14)

I have never been in prison – either for something I have done or for something I have not done. I can remember once in primary school being wrongly accused of being unkind to a new boy who had distorted features. It was a false accusation, but I was still regarded as guilty, and that hurt!

In our present world, it is sadly very common for Christians to be punished for things they have not done. In Muslim areas, a person has only to criticize a Christian for allegedly saying or doing something against that faith to ensure that that person will be treated harshly. Even if the Christian gets out of prison, he will still be living under suspicion, and so it may no longer be safe for him to remain in that community.

Paul is writing this letter from prison. It is not that he has done anything wrong: he is imprisoned because there are those who object to his preaching of the gospel.

The important thing here is the attitude that he takes. He could have felt very sorry for himself, but that is not the case. In fact, he looks at the positive results of his imprisonment.

In verse 12 he writes: "Now I want you to know, brothers and sisters, that what has happened to me has actually served to advance the gospel."

Paul's enemies thought that putting this preacher in jail would put an end to his missionary work, but it had exactly the opposite effect. In the verses that follow, Paul shows how this works out in practice.

(1) The Effect on Paul

No doubt, Paul was not the only one in jail. There must have been others there who were guilty of theft, violence and a variety of other culpable offences. When people saw them in prison, they were aware that they had been put there because they had broken the law.

Paul, however, stood out. He was not guilty of any of these offences. His 'crime' was that he was a follower of Christ, and that he tried to persuade others to turn to Christ also. In the past, before Christ had turned his life around, he himself had arrested others for that very crime. This was particularly obvious to the palace guard. They were used to taking care of prisoners, and in their time they had come across all types. For the most part these would be hardened criminals who simply got what they deserved. Their behaviour would also yield ample evidence for this.

But how were they to assess Paul? He had not taken part in any kind of criminal offence. Even though he was in prison, he did not have a belligerent attitude. He was a model citizen – apart from the fact that he had declared himself a follower of Jesus Christ. Some of them were bound to be curious about him. This man's loyalty to Christ must be very great if he was willing to accept imprisonment for the sake of it. Some of them may have considered what it might be like if they too were to follow Christ. This man's dedication was so attractive.

From Paul's point of view, this was also a new opportunity for witness. In the normal course of events, he would be unable to preach the Gospel to Roman soldiers. But when he is in prison, handcuffed to different soldiers in turn, he has a captive audience. God can turn any circumstance into something positive.

There are many situations today when Christians find themselves in prison for their faith. Often this would be in a place where a militant form of Islam is in control. There are many stories of such Christians continuing to make their faith known to others, even though they are in jail, and sometimes the prison staff become converts, even though it is to their own peril. This is because they have seen something authentic in the lives of such prisoners.

I do not speak of situations where Christians have behaved foolishly and brought this punishment upon themselves, but only when it is faithfulness to God which has led their enemies to imprison them. For a Christian to remain loyal to God when undergoing such unjust treatment can be a powerful act of witness.

(2) Other Effects

There was a second positive result of his imprisonment. He writes, "And, because of my chains, most of the brothers and sisters have become confident in the Lord and dare all the more to proclaim the gospel without fear".

Looked at from a merely human standpoint, Paul's imprisonment ought to have had the opposite effect. Fear of their own arrest might have persuaded other believers to stay quiet about their faith.

We do not have this problem in our own country. It is true that some Christians may be taken to court because they have made choices at work based on their deep Christian convictions, they may lose their job, but they are not likely to be imprisoned because of this.

It is so different for Christians in so many parts of the world. Until recently, the main opposing force was Communism. In Russia, many Christians would be imprisoned for their faith; though one Communist admitted, "Kill one Christian and six more spring up." In China the situation has eased and the Church has grown remarkably; nevertheless there are still many instances of Christians being ill treated because of their faith and sadly, this tendency is growing again under the leadership of the present 'dictator'. In North Korea, however, the most dangerous place in the world to be a Christian, one word about your faith to others might lead to yourself and various generations of your family being sent to a severe labour camp. Yet, even under such circumstances, Christians continue to follow Jesus.

The greatest threat these days against Christians is militant Islam. In North Nigeria, Syria and many other places Islamic terrorists kill Christians under the conviction that they are showing loyalty to their own faith. The wonder is that Christians continue to pursue their faith despite the dangers. It is as if, when Christians are placed in such dangerous situations, God gives them extra strength to carry on. He also takes away their fear.

By contrast, in our own country, the Church often appears weak and ineffective. Here we are not persecuted for our faith. There is no great cost facing us. In a situation of ease, we have grown weak and ineffective. When people look at us, they do not see vibrant Christians whose lives challenge them. The devil knows that decline in Christian standards is of more effect here than mere persecution.

Over the next few years it could become more and more difficult to maintain Christians standards in Western society. If true Christians are willing to make a stand for the truth, despite opposition, we could even find ourselves in the position here described by Paul, and there could be an upward turn in the Church's fortunes, a journey from decline into renewal.

Is there an element of cost in my own Christian life?

Chapter 6
PREACHING THE GOSPEL
(1:15-18A)

Churches can vary very much. As a boy I attended a church school, and because of this I got attached to a particular church in the centre of my town. It was well attended, and when large conferences, especially political ones, were held in the town, that was the church its members went to on the Sunday. At the age of 14 I was confirmed (through my senior school) and henceforth I began to attend the services weekly because that was the thing to do. Although my faith did not touch me at a deep level, I took seriously my attachment to that church.

It was only when I had to do National Service that I met up with Christians who claimed to be 'born again' and came to such a personal commitment myself. From then onwards I called myself an Evangelical Christian.

When my National Service was ending, the Vicar of my home church died. I prayed that God would send an Evangelical. He responded by sending an Evangelical vicar and an Evangelical curate, both from Northern Ireland.

When we look at the wider church, we discover there is no one thing that binds all of them together except loyalty to the same God. Some are Evangelical, some are Anglo Catholic, some are liberal, and some would not be able to tell you what they are.

Even the ones that call themselves Evangelical may vary. The term comes from the word for 'gospel', but now we have Conservative Evangelical, Liberal Evangelical and a host of types for which it would be hard to attach a fitting name. There are churches which would not use the name 'Evangelical', yet their aim is also to preach the Gospel to outsiders. What is important is that, one way or another, we are telling people the good news that God wants to save them.

The diocese in Northern Ireland where I live has a link diocese in the USA. It is an Anglo Catholic diocese; yet I have observed there is a strong desire to bring people to Christ, which we would normally associate with good Evangelicals.

Paul here is talking about the preaching of the Gospel. Sometimes it is preached in what seem to be highly commendable ways, but at other times the methods might seem highly suspect. What are we to do about this?

In the next few verses Paul describes two groups of people who preach the Gospel, but in very different ways.

(1) Out of Envy and Rivalry

The first group preach Christ out of envy and rivalry. They have selfish ambitions and they are not sincere. Their aim is to stir up trouble for Paul while he is in prison. Now it is hard to see how anyone can preach the Gospel with the aim of deliberately stirring up trouble for a good leader. What, then, does he mean here? It looks as if these people were envious of Paul and his success. He had already won many converts. They wanted to enjoy their own success, and they felt they could only do this by acting as clear rivals to Paul. They wanted to attract a lot of followers to themselves and to their way of doing things. If their work should get Paul into trouble, they were happy enough with such an outcome.

How easy it is for churches to behave this way in our own day! The main aim is not to bring others into salvation but to get a good personal following. Of course, the two may both happen at the same time, but their motivation is suspect. Churches of different denominations, instead of working together, merely seek to win personal success.

Happily in our own day there are such things as Alpha courses, which are widely used right across the denominations.

This is one of the brightest tendencies at the present time. But in some villages, towns and cities, one particular church seems to regard itself as the sole purveyor of the Gospel and refuses to cooperate with churches of other denominations to further the work of the Gospel. They may be highly successful churches, but they are woefully blinkered.

Let us see ourselves as partners with other churches where the Gospel is preached and not as rivals.

(2) Out of Goodwill and Love

The second group preach the Gospel out of goodwill and love. We want the best for others, and this stems from love. Presumably this means first of all a love for God, but it should then extend to a love for the people to whom they preach. But the specific reference here is to their love for Paul. They do not see him as a rival who happens to have a bigger success rate than they do. They are happy simply to work with him in bringing the Gospel to others. Who was it that brought you to Christ in the first place? It may just have been part of a long process; or there may be an individual to whom you can look back with thanksgiving. Then, of course, you will think of that person with love and gratitude. You may also think of others who have helped you along at various stages of your Christian life. Obviously you will love them, but in the context of a love which is primarily for God himself.

Some of us may be called 'professionals'. We have been ordained into the ministry of the Church and belong to a particular denomination. But we are not trying to promote our denomination above others, nor are we trying to enhance our own personal standing: it is the exaltation of Christ that matters most.

(3) Attitude to Both Groups

We would have expected Paul to condemn the one group and praise the other, but that is not what he does. What matters to him is that the Gospel is preached, whether it should be from good or bad motives. God can even use imperfect churches for the carrying out of his purposes.

Sometimes there is rivalry amongst churches. Some think they are the only ones who preach the Gospel in the right way. But there are churches of very different backgrounds which give a faithful presentation of the Gospel. I am not talking about churches which have very different priorities that are unrelated to the Gospel, but to those which are committed to sharing the Good News. We may see others, then, not as rivals, but as partners in the sharing of the Gospel.

Let us take a look at our own motives. Are we trying to enjoy a bigger success rate than other churches, or are we content to preach the Gospel faithfully and to leave the rest with God? Secondly, what is our attitude to Jesus Christ? Do we put him first, so that it is not we or our church that gets the glory, but Jesus himself?

At the end of this section we do not find Paul shaking his head with frustration in the light of such negative features. Instead he is full of rejoicing. That is the way we should feel as a part of God's team: to bring the Gospel to outsiders we should rejoice that Christ is being preached, even when the circumstances do not tick all the right boxes.

What motivation do I have for making the Gospel known to others?

Chapter 7
A GOOD OUTCOME
(1:18B-20)

"Why is this happening to me?" Do we ever ask such a question? Maybe we have started a new job. At the beginning we had high hopes. Before long, however, we find ourselves faced with unexpected opposition, and it becomes harder to maintain our equilibrium. Did we get things wrong? Or is God working out his purpose in a way we did not expect?

Paul has already indicated that he is, at the time of writing, undergoing imprisonment. He could have assumed that this meant that God had deserted him; but he does not see it that way. Instead of feeling miserable he is full of rejoicing, for he is looking not at his own unfortunate circumstances but at the way the Gospel is being proclaimed.

It is unlikely that you are in prison as you read this, though for many Christians today in other parts of the world this is a grim reality. However, you may be facing other negative circumstances, such as recurring illness, financial upheaval, recent bereavement or a host of other misfortunes.

Although Paul is currently in a negative situation, he looks at two positive outcomes. These are not merely passive outcomes, for he believes that God has a positive purpose in all this. When things go wrong for us, it is only too easy to take a negative view of things, so we have much to learn from Paul in these verses. Here he looks first at his circumstances and then at his attitude.

(1) His Circumstances

Concerning his circumstances, the first thing he looks for is vindication. He says in verse 19: "I know that through your prayers and God's provision of the Spirit of Jesus Christ what has happened to me will turn out for my deliverance."

He is confident of his deliverance for two reasons. The first is the prayers of God's people. He may feel alone as he languishes in his cell with only a Roman soldier for company, but he knows there are many fellow-Christians, currently invisible to him, who are praying for him, and he has the assurance that God will answer their prayers by setting him free.

The second is the presence of the Holy Spirit. We are not trying to accomplish things through merely human means. We have a power beyond ourselves in which to trust – that of the Holy Spirit. What seems impossible to man is possible to God.

I used to enjoy reading the novels of A. J. Cronin. In many of his novels we would witness a young man, usually a doctor, facing all kinds of opposition; but by the end of the novel all can see that he has been right after all. Such novels have a 'feel good factor'.

In real life, however, things do not always work out so perfectly. We are following what we believe is the right way, but all we meet with is opposition and failure. In my times of prayer I often find myself informed about faithful Christian witnesses in the many troubled parts of the world, who constantly face opposition that could lead to imprisonment, attack or even death. If I were one of them, could I face my troubles with the same faith that Paul did? The quick answer is that it is not for us to know unless we are actually in that situation. God gives us help not for imaginary situations, but for real ones.

Several decades ago I remember reading about the experiences of Geoffrey Bull under Communists in Tibet. He suffered great rigours in prison, but God ministered to him. Eventually he was released, but he confessed that, even if this had not happened, he would have been grateful for the way in which God used this experience to deepen his inner life.

Paul believes that, as a result of prayer and the work of the Holy Spirit, he will be set free; but we get the impression that, even if this did not happen, he would not abandon his trust in God.

(2) His Attitude

Now we turn to look at his attitude. First of all he says he expects that he will not be ashamed. It is all to easy to feel ashamed if we have dabbled in sin of any kind; but Paul speaks of another kind of shame. Some people are ashamed of being seen as a Christian because it might mean that others take a negative view of this and so make life difficult for them. It is only too easy to disguise our faith so that we do not have to encounter such an attitude. In Romans 1:16 he says: "I am not ashamed of the gospel, because it is the power of God that brings salvation."

Paul goes on to say that he wants to show courage. In wartime we admire soldiers who show courage and even award medals to them. The reference here, however, is to the courage of Christians. I sometimes wonder what I would be like if I was facing martyrdom. Sometimes we see the bravery of Christians in our own day as they face execution for their faith. Sadly, this is currently a very widespread situation. Going back a few centuries, we may think of Cranmer at the stake stretching his hand into the fire, for it was through this hand he had in a time of spiritual decline signed a recantation.

But we are to show courage not merely as we face death but in a whole variety of situations. I accepted Jesus as my Saviour when I was doing National Service in the RAF. A friend of mine was keen on scouting, and I agreed to give a hand. When we were on a day trip one of the boys invited us to take a look at a den which he had established. Thus I found myself scrambling along a narrow ledge with a sheer drop below. At a human level I was not at all comfortable with this, but I felt God was giving me courage to face this without fear.

However, Paul's courage is mainly to be seen in the light of a surrounding world which does not readily accept Christians and their standards. It is especially difficult to make a stance for Christ if you are a young person surrounded by friends and acquaintances who scoff at the Christian life and all it stands for.

Paul is eager that Christ should be exalted in his body, whether that means life or death for him. I sometimes read about Christians working in a land where there is a lot of opposition to the Gospel. When the situation becomes dangerous for missionaries, they are urged to pull out. Many do, but there are still some who feel it is right to remain. Would I be brave enough to do that? I do not know, for I have never been placed in that sort of a situation.

We may not be in danger of martyrdom, but we may have to face misunderstanding, rejection, ostracism, criticism and other such negative attitudes. Are we so loyal to God that we will remain faithful to him and his standards even when there is great cost?

The Christian life is not for weaklings; but any courage which we display in following a dangerous course comes not from our own innate strength but directly from God himself.

If I am facing opposition, how do I handle it?

Chapter 8
OF LIFE AND DEATH
(1:21-6)

Recently I was watching a programme about terminal illness. Twelve people were shown, all of whom had learned that they only had a short time to live. Sadly, only one of them claimed to have a Christian faith and therefore to be able to look forward to a richer life in the next world.

That is what Paul is speaking of here. As a persecuted believer, it is quite possible he may face martyrdom. He summarises his position by saying, "For me, to live is Christ, and to die is gain." Let us look at those two conditions.

(1) Staying Alive

What would it mean for Paul to stay alive? He tells us in the next verse that, if his life is prolonged, he will be able to do more fruitful work. We know that Paul worked hard to bring the Gospel to as many people as possible: this was his lifelong passion.

Personally I can thank God for giving me a long life. Although I am 81 years old at the time of writing, by God's grace I am still strong in mind and body and can therefore still be of service to God.

When Paul looks at his own life and accepts that he is going to live longer on this earth, he is not looking for his own wellbeing. Many people who have no faith simply want to prolong their life on earth as much as possible. It is all for their own pleasure and comfort. On the other hand, there are some people who suffer poor health and they would like to die just to get rid of the pain and discomfort, even though they do not have anything to look forward to afterwards.

Paul is happy to live longer if he can thus bring benefit to other people. He says in verse 25: "and I will continue with all of you for your progress and joy in the faith". His great gift is that of teaching others about the faith; and as he teaches others he is able to observe their spiritual progress. If he were to die early, he would not be able to have such an ongoing and positive spiritual effect on others.

He continues with the words: "so that through my being with you again your boasting in Christ Jesus will abound on account of me". It is not so much a matter of filling others with spiritual knowledge as of furthering their relationship with Christ. He does not want them to boast of himself as their teacher but rather of Christ, to whom they really belong.

It will mean a lot of hard work, and it can entail rough treatment at the hands of the authorities, but if it means that more people will enjoy a close relationship with Christ, that is what Paul is looking for most of all. If he were taken to heaven early, he would no longer be able help others to build up their relationship with Christ. He is therefore content to stay alive somewhat longer so that this precious work may go on.

Most of us would not have such a deep spiritual effect on others as Paul had. He talks here about 'fruitful labour'. Nevertheless we all have work to do for God, and while we are alive we may gladly give ourselves to it. Whether our contribution is small or large, and whatever form it takes, we can all have a positive effect on others.

Length of life, on its own, is not necessarily something positive. Hezekiah was given an extra fifteen years of life by God; but he lacked the zeal of his early years, and he became boastful, showing off his riches to visitors. In his case, it would have been better to have died earlier, while his faith was stronger.

If Paul is granted a longer life, he wants to put it to good use. He wants to work among the Philippians in such a way that their boasting in Christ Jesus will abound" (v. 26). He is not thinking of his own benefit but of that which others can enjoy.

There is no guarantee that, if our life is prolonged, it will be easy. Paul speaks here of suffering for God. In our own day many Christians in other parts of the world have to endure a lot of suffering because of their faith. Because they know and love God, they are ready to endure this. How would we feel if we had the same choice?

(2)   Giving Up His Life

Prolonging our life is not necessarily a good thing. I read recently that a large number of children born today will live to be 100. So what? It is not the length of our life that matters but the quality. If we live well into old age, but plagued with sickness and boredom, what good does this do to us?

To Paul, however, death comes not just as a termination but as an exciting new beginning. He says: "to die is gain" and "I desire to depart and be with Christ, which is better by far".

The best thing we can do in our present life is to grow in the knowledge of Jesus Christ; but we still live among many distractions and hindrances. In the next life we shall know him more fully and there will be nothing to take us from him. That is why Paul is so eager to pass through the portal of death in order to enter into this better experience.

I suspect that not many of us look forward so eagerly to death. We like to hold on to our life and to our earthly relationships for as long as we can. Many of those who want to die have the wrong reasons for this. It is because they hate the life they are living and see no reason to remain alive. There are others, who, understandably, long for death because of severe illness. For the Christian, however, the quality of our present life is not the main issue: it is the quality of the life to come that matters most.

Those of us who have driven a car with small children as passengers will have heard the question, "Are we nearly there yet?" The children are so much looking forward to some new adventure that they find it hard to wait. Yet how many of us as adults look forward to the next life with such a level of expectation?

It is not because we are tired of this life and desire to get away from it (though there are some for whom this is true); it is rather that the quality of the life to come is so much greater that we are longing to enter into the experience. For the time being, however, we must wait. There is no justification for suicide. We have to wait for the time of

God's choosing. We may die suddenly and unexpectedly, or we may die after a long illness. It is not for us to choose. All we know is that, however death comes to us, it will be the start of a wonderful new life.

There is, of course, one important proviso. We have to know Christ in our present life. If we have lived without him, how can we be assured that we shall enjoy his presence in the life to come? Paul lives in Christ's presence in the current life, but he knows it will be far better when he is in heaven.

Do we share his attitude toward life and death?

Am I happy to leave the length of my life in the Lord's hands?

Chapter 9
LIVING LIVES WORTHY OF THE GOSPEL
(1:27-30)

Paul has been talking about his own attitude to life and death; but now he turns back to consider the situation of the Philippians themselves. He is concerned that they should live good Christian lives.

In verse 27 he writes: "Whatever happens, conduct yourselves in a manner worthy of the Gospel of Christ." Their behaviour matters.

Doctrine and practice belong together. Some people may seem faultless in their understanding of Christian doctrine, but their lives may not be much affected by it. Others may behave better, but they do not have much understanding of Christian teaching. Neither position is satisfactory. Our good moral behaviour is meant to stem from our understanding of God's truth.

As a UK citizen, when I travel overseas I am a kind of ambassador for my country. When others see the way I behave, it will affect their impression of what British people are like. That is why it is disturbing to read of young people who become known for their riotous behaviour when holidaying far from home.

We are ambassadors of the Lord Jesus Christ. People will look at our lives, and this should affect what they think of Jesus, whom we claim to represent.

Paul goes on to give us three pictures in order to illustrate this.

(1) Cooperation

First we have a picture of cooperation. We may call ourselves Christians through the cooperation of Father and Son in procuring our salvation, and it is the Spirit who works in harmony with them in making our salvation clear to us.

Paul is eager for news of them, so that he may see how this is working out in their own lives. He knows they cannot stand firm if they are simply trusting in their own abilities, but that they have to rely on the Holy Spirit to help them.

But they are not just individuals. They are part of the Christian community, and it is up to them to cooperate in making the gospel known.

Two pictures are used here to describe our Christian stance. The first is that of standing firm. The second is that of fighting for the Gospel.

If a soldier finds himself on boggy ground, which gives him a poor footing, it is hard to fight properly. So the more firmly we understand the Gospel and are strengthened by the Spirit, the better we shall be able to strive for God's truth amongst unbelievers.

We are to fight together as one. When Christians are divided about what they believe and how they should behave, they make little impact on the world outside. This does not mean that we are all carbon copies of each other. We all have different ideas and ways of behaving and our personalities may differ widely; but we are agreed on essentials. When this is so, we are more likely to have a positive impact on the world around us.

For some people, however, the fight is hard. In so many parts of the world, if you claim to be a Christian and if you strive to witness to others, you are seen as a threat. What do you do if you are a pastor and you are told you must not lead worship any more? What do you do if a single word about your faith can lead to imprisonment or even to death?

At least, they don't have to do it alone. They are more able to stand firm when there are other Christians who are facing the same problems. Such cooperation is vital if Christians are to have an effective witness to the unbelieving world.

(2) Fearlessness

Secondly we have a picture of fearlessness. In verse 28 Paul says that these Christians are not afraid in any way of those who oppose them. The word translated 'frightened' in the NIV is a strong word. It could even be translated with the word 'terrified'.

For most of us, this is foreign to our experience. If people oppose our faith, it does not lead us unto danger; rather are we more likely to be treated with indifference.

Ralph Martin, in his commentary, suggests that the thought is of mob violence. Sadly, this is very common in our world today. In many places the Christian minority are in danger of violent attack, which could lead to many deaths. If we were placed in such a situation, how loyal to God would we be? Maybe it is hard to answer that until it falls within our experience.

Are we to suppose, then, that this verse has nothing to say to us in a situation that is not fraught with danger? Not so. In both situations, the main enemy is Satan. It is he who opposes our faith and all that we stand for. We may not be in physical danger, but we may still be scorned by those who hold to secular views and treated as oddities. In fact, opposition here in the West to those who take a clear Christian stance is growing. Both evil words and indifference have the power to hurt us. We hear of people even losing their jobs because they have adopted a Christian position on some issue.

Their very capacity to withstand such opposition is a positive sign. They could not have made such a stance without divine help. When people oppose us for our Christian stance it is, sadly, a sign that they will be destroyed (unless they do a U turn) but that we shall be saved. Opposition, then, may have positive as well as negative effects. We stand not before human courts but the court of God.

(3) Suffering

Thirdly we have a picture of suffering. God does not promise that Christians will be excused suffering. Some of our suffering is what we share with the rest of mankind; but there is also another kind of suffering which stems from reaction to our Christian faith. It is this latter kind of suffering which is described here.

When we turn to Christ, we receive great benefits, but that does not protect us from suffering while we are in this world. In this verse it even appears to be regarded as a privilege. It is one that Paul himself enjoyed, and it is the experience of believers throughout the world in our own day.

This is the suffering that comes from serving Christ faithfully in this world. There are some who, in bearing witness to their faith, act unwisely and bring upon themselves a different kind of suffering. This is not to be commended. True Christian suffering stems from our faithful allegiance to Christ. There is a suffering that comes from natural disasters such as earthquakes, famine and so on; but that is not being spoken of here.

For most of the people reading this the suffering of Christians is something we read about as happening in other parts of the world, especially where a religion such as Islam, Hinduism or Buddhism is prominent. Compared with this, we suffer very little.

In what ways, then, may we expect to suffer? Maybe because of our faith we are left out of friendship circles, not considered for promotion, opposed by family members, or misunderstood by those who do not understand our motives. In a host of ways, we may be regarded as oddities, who do not fit into the normal patterns of society. This may not sound like severe persecution, but it can still be hurtful.

When we suffer, it makes us feel caught up in a struggle, but we were never promised that to be a Christian is to live a life where there are no challenges.

Paul himself is no stranger to such suffering and so he can encourage others by his own example. Now, after describing his own life as a Christian, he turns in the next chapter to observe the central place occupied by Jesus Christ.

What does it cost you to take your stand as a Christian?

Chapter 10
SOME CHRISTIAN QUALITIES
(2:1)

A short while before her death, my wife had a vision for the churches of our area. At the time, each church fellowship met regularly merely on its own premises, but there was little involvement with people from other churches. As a result of her concern, we began to meet together twice a year, and the result has been holding services packed with enthusiastic worshippers of different ages and backgrounds. She was also concerned that the local clergy would have more contact with one another. The clergy now meet together regularly to share fellowship and to plan combined events. We feel that in doing this we are also offering one another mutual support.

Here at the start of the second chapter of Philippians, Paul is talking primarily about unity. What is it that unites us?

One of the barriers to such unity is thinking too much of ourselves. Sadly, there are churches which will not join with the rest of us, presumably because they think they have got things right and do not need any contribution from other churches. In other words, they lack that humility which we need to show both as individuals and as churches if we are to learn from one another.

All this depends on how we relate to Christ himself. At the start of this chapter we have a string of reasons which should lead us into this positive attitude to our fellow Christians. That is what we shall look at in this chapter.

Here are some qualities, then, that we should be showing.

(1) Unity

First of all we have the encouragement of being united with Christ. This makes the Church different from any other organisation. We may be linked with others because we all support the same football team, because we have a common concern for the treatment of cancer patients, because we believe our political party will have the best contribution to make to our society, because we all appreciate the same kind of music, because we wish to improve the quality of our environment and so on. In other words, we have common interests, and some of these show a genuine commitment to good. However, what links us as Christians is not our common interests but our common commitment: we are committed to Christ himself, and that special relationship somehow makes us different.

Jesus speaks of this in John 17:22, where he says, "I have given them the glory that you gave me, that they may be one as we are one."

If each of us is personally committed to Christ, this gives us also a special relationship with one another. He is our head, and all we want to do is to serve, obey and reflect him. We are in a sense brothers and sisters. We are organically related to him. If that is how we feel, we shall want to understand one another and to work together for him in this world.

(2) Comfort

Secondly, we know comfort through his love for us. Love is a potent force. In a good marriage, it is the love between husband and wife that leads to true contentment and agreement. That love also affects the way they relate to their children. Love is a potent force.

Here, however, we are talking about Christ's love for us. He loved us so much that he died for us. How much more deeply than that could he have revealed his love? In Romans 5:8 we read "But God demonstrates his own love for us in this: While we were still sinners, Christ died for us". You cannot show any greater love for another person than by dying for them. That is how much Christ loves us. We also read in Ephesians 5:25: that "Christ loved the church and gave himself up for her".

46

If we are all recipients of the same love of Christ, how ought this to affect our mutual relationships? That is what Paul is writing about here. We love one another as close family.

Furthermore, love is not just an emotion, it gives us harmony with one another and removes any suspicion of rivalry. It does not mean that our lives will always follow a smooth pattern, but we are given the ability to handle any difficulties that may arise.

(3) The Holy Spirit

Thirdly we have a common experience of the Holy Spirit. It is not different spirits that lie within us but the same Holy Spirit whom God gives to every true believer. This experience binds us together. We are reminded of Ephesians 4:3, where we read "Make every effort to keep the unity of the Spirit through the bond of peace".

Sadly, in our own day, it is often different attitudes toward the Holy Spirit that keep churches apart from one another rather than uniting them. Some, for instance, would teach that if you cannot speak in tongues you do not have the Spirit. The truth is that the Spirit may give different gifts to different people and may be manifested in different forms of worship, but it is not his role to keep Christians apart from their fellows. The Spirit is meant to bind us together. It is the Spirit who enables us to express our true unity. Whether we call ourselves charismatic or not is unimportant, as long as we are open to all that the Spirit wants to do in our lives. In our diversity we also embrace a unity.

(4) Tenderness and Compassion

Fourthly we are to show tenderness and compassion. When we relate to others it is not on a superficial level. We seek to understand them, their good points and their faults, without any sense of harshness, and then to reflect the love of Jesus in the way we relate to them. We feel along with them: that is what compassion is all about - it is a feeling with others. They see us as people who love and understand them and to whom they can come for help. When outsiders see how we relate to one another, does this put them off the Christian faith, or does this help them to see how genuine relationships are among those who love the Lord?

In this verse, then, Paul has been giving the various incentives that will help Christians to live together as the true people of God. In the next three verses he will show us how this all works out in practice.

Would the ways we relate together as Christians in our local church have a positive effect on outsiders?

Chapter 11
HOW WE RELATE TO OTHERS
(2:2-4)

The Christian faith is a very practical religion. It is not just a matter of what goes on in the head, but it has to be worked out in practice and especially in our relationships with others.

However, if we are to relate properly to others we must first relate to God in the way described in the previous chapter.

Now Paul wants to see evidence that God is working in them, an evidence which will personally give him joy. He goes on to speak of those qualities which he will look for in them as the result of this.

(1) Likemindedness

We see this in verse 2. Paul really cares about this. If they show this characteristic and those which follow, then it will give him a lot of joy.

Being likeminded does not mean that we have the same viewpoint on everything. We are not carbon copies of one another. It would be very boring if we all thought exactly the same way as our fellow Christians and there was never any exchange of ideas. It would be boring too if we all had exactly the same hobbies. What it means is that we should be of a common purpose in the way we serve God.

Look round any congregation, and you will see variety : there are differences in our interests, our abilities, our appearance, our circumstances and so on, but we should be at one in our commitment to the Lord and to his purpose for us.

In verse 5 we shall be told that we must have the same mind as Jesus Christ, but before we come to that, let us look at the details given here.

Our unity with one another is demonstrated in three ways.

First we have the same love for one another, which is a reflection of Christ's love for us. This is not just something in head and heart, but shows itself in the way we behave toward our fellow Christians. It is not sexual love, but a divinely inspired love. This love should have a profound effect on how we think and act when we are with them.

Secondly, we should be one in spirit. We rely on the same Holy Spirit to guide us and this encourages us to see things from the same spiritual point of view. This does not mean we are always agreed on all matters, but it means that in all things we want to put Christ first rather than simply trying to put our own ideas into practice.

Thirdly we must be of one mind – that does not mean, as we have already seen, we have identical thoughts about everything, but it means we are ready to share our thoughts with others, that we are able to resolve potential conflict and reach a common God-given agreement. So we are not carbon copies of one another but, despite our individual differences, are heading in the same direction.

(2) Humility

Secondly we read about humility in verse 3. We are told not to do anything from selfish ambition. This does not mean that all ambition is wrong. It would be a poor thing if all Christians were determined to remain in their current situation because they lacked drive and initiative. It is good to have motivation for forging ahead. To have a life without any ambition would be very dull indeed. The difference is in what lies behind that ambition. Are we looking to God to do new things in our lives, or are we simply governed by our own desire to achieve a higher position? So it is not ambition that is wrong, but seeking to make ourselves great rather than reflecting God's greatness.

Sometimes the progress of a church can be stifled because of someone who thinks only of his own ambitions. There was once a church where I was curate that had a very conservative churchwarden.

If we tried to do anything new, he would stifle it. His ambition was to keep the church exactly as it was, and therefore to thwart any plans the Lord might have for its progress. The minister himself must also ensure that he is following the Lord and not just pursuing his own personal projects.

We are told that in humility we should value others above ourselves. In our planning we are not trying to exalt ourselves. We are therefore ready to listen to others and take their suggestions into account. This does not mean, however, that we always give in to their demands, for both they and we are subject to the Lord's governance. However, we are more concerned for their interests than for our own.

I am reminded here of Romans 12:3: 'Do not think of yourself more highly then you ought, but rather think of yourself with sober judgment, in accordance with the faith God has distributed to each of you.'. Let us be honest, then, in our self-appraisal.

(3)   Empathy

Thirdly we have empathy with others. Verse 4 reads: "not looking to your own interests but each of you to the interests of others".

There is a sense in which we are looking to our own interests and rightly so. That does not mean we are looking for our own comfort or our own prosperity. But surely it is perfectly in order to want to become the best that we can be, especially in a moral and spiritual sense.

However, in more ordinary features, we put the needs of others before our own needs. In very simple terms, it may mean taking the smaller piece of cake rather than the larger one when food is being offered. It may mean paying the bill ourselves for a meal which two of us have both enjoyed. It may mean letting the other person have the credit for something we have really done together. These, however, are very limited suggestions.

In reality this goes well beyond looking to each other's material needs. We have spiritual needs as well. We want our friends to get closer to God and to appreciate his blessings more.

So, imitating the humility of Christ includes putting others before ourselves and rejoicing at their success.

To what extent do I value other people?

Chapter 12
THE INCARNATION OF JESUS
(2:5-7)

We do not have to work out for ourselves what our thinking should be like as Christians, for we have the example of Jesus Christ himself. We are told, therefore, in verse 5: "In your relationships with one another, have the same mindset as Jesus Christ".

Of course, when we look at how Jesus behaved when he was on earth, we may observe two opposites. On the one hand he was humble: he allowed himself to be ill treated and even to be flogged and crucified. On the other hand he claimed to be the Son of God and this showed in his authoritative teaching. It is the first of these that we are called to emulate.

In these verses we see four traits in his character while on earth.

(1) Renunciation

At first verse 6 sounds mystifying. We read: "Who, being in very nature God, did not consider equality with God something to be used to his own advantage"

It has never happened before or since: a man walked this earth who was actually in essence the God who made everything. He could have persuaded others selfishly of his divine origin and reaped for himself privileges galore; but that was not why he came to earth.

One feature of King George VI that is still remembered was the way in which he behaved during the Second World War. He could have left London and gone to live somewhere safer; but he stayed there despite the bombing, and he visited bomb sites in order to identify with his people.

Jesus could have led a privileged life, but what good would that have done? How could he then have set people free from their sin and guilt? Instead of that, he lived with very little of this world's resources and came to a terrible end on the Cross. He never ceased to be the Son of God, and he demonstrated that in his teaching and miracles; but in his ordinary living he behaved in a very humble manner.

We may also compare Adam and Christ. Adam began as a privileged human being, but through his act of disobedience he brought condemnation to his descendants. Jesus, though identified with fallen man, by one great act of obedience brought restoration for man.

There are a number of people in history, and not just Christians, who have renounced their personal privileges in order to help others. Buddha left his family and friends, with all their wealth, in order to seek for the truth as he would understand it. C.T. Studd, a wealthy young heir, Cambridge graduate and England cricket captain, left all this behind to serve God first in China and later in India and Africa.

Most of those reading this book will, I expect, come from perfectly ordinary backgrounds; yet we may have had, in some smaller way, to renounce our own privileges in order to serve God in humbler circumstances. It is not privilege but obedience which determines the kind of people we become.

(2)   Self-emptying

After speaking of Christ's qualities, Paul goes on to say in verse 7 : "he made himself nothing". The technical word for this self-emptying is 'kenosis'. It does not mean that Jesus gave up his divinity when he became man; but, though he was still God, he accepted all the limitations which his assumption of our humanity imposed on him. So for that time there would be no omniscience or omnipotence. These qualities still belonged to God but not to his incarnate self.

However, Jesus still had more knowledge than the ordinary human being. Even as a boy of 12, when visiting the Temple, he surprised the teachers there because of the extent of his knowledge. When speaking with the Samaritan woman, he knew that she had had five husbands.

He knew about the coin in the fish's mouth. In such instances, then, he had special knowledge; but, then, there are people filled with the Spirit who have such knowledge, but would not admit themselves to be divine.

All we can see is that Jesus laid aside everything that would stop him living a privileged human life on earth. This must have been very costly. He had to lay aside all that splendour and lead a simple life that was marked by suffering.

Some of us, in order to serve God, may have to set aside other ambitions, friendships and skills, since they do not fit in with God's plans for us; but none of us will have to give up as much as Jesus himself did.

As a Cambridge graduate, it is conceivable that I might have been able to secure a job that would have brought in a lot of money; but I sensed that God was calling me into the ministry of the Church, and that is the profession I followed. But that was a small sacrifice when compared with that of Christ himself.

(3)   Service

Jesus took the nature of a servant. That is not what the wise men expected when they looked for the new born king. They looked for him in the king's palace, but found that he had been born in a stable.

We think of the 'Suffering Servant' found in Isaiah. In the four passages devoted to this material, we see Jesus as the one who took the form of a servant in order that by his death he might bring us forgiveness for all our sins.

If Jesus, despite his origins, was ready to be called a servant, what does this mean for us? It is all too easy to look for high position, power and respect. That is very different from the role of a servant. Yet, if we would be like Jesus, it involves a great degree of humility. Like him, we should be ready to serve God and to serve other people without looking for great rewards for ourselves.

(4) Identification

Jesus was made in the likeness of man. That was not pretence: he actually became one of us. When people saw him, they saw God and man at the same time. Even becoming fully human entailed great sacrifice, to say nothing of the suffering and death which were to follow.

Paul spoke about becoming all things to all men. In other words, we are to identify with those around us so that we are in a good position to help them. But it was Jesus who started it all. It does not mean that we try to copy others, but we want to get as close to them as we can so as to share our faith with them.

When Hudson Taylor started to wear Chinese dress, he was scorned by other missionaries; but later it was seen as a wise move, as local Chinese could see him as 'one of them'.

So we have seen something here of the mind of Christ; now we shall go on to look at his ministry.

What have we given up in order to live as better Christians?

Chapter 13
THE MINISTRY OF JESUS
(2:8)

The passage we are studying here is thought to be an old Christian hymn. It certainly contains great truths about Jesus Christ for us to reflect on. In this section we shall consider four things about him that are to be found in this verse.

(1) Manhood

It says here that he was found in appearance as a man. Let us not underestimate what this verse is saying. It does not mean he only looked like a man: it means he really did become one of us. Let us compare his experience with ours so as to validate the statement.

1. As a man, he experienced growth from childhood, through boyhood and adolescence until he became an adult human being. It was the same sort of growth which we also experience.

2. As a man he shared the same needs as we do. For instance, he knew hunger and thirst: once he asked a Samaritan woman for a drink of water. When tired, he went with his disciples to find a place to rest. If we are tempted to complain about our human condition, let us recall that Jesus shared it completely, and that included the same senses of need.

3. As a man, he suffered temptation as we do. We are familiar with the story of his three temptations in the wilderness; but we must not suppose that this was the only time he was tempted. We are told in Hebrews 4:15 that he was tempted in every way that we are, but did not sin. So when we are tempted we know that he is there to help us, for he knows what we are going through. There is no need to feel guilty about being tempted – only when we give in to it does it become a sin.

4. As a man, he died. We are all subject to mortality and Jesus, in his human condition, shared this. Sometimes we shudder at the temporary nature of our life on earth and the inevitable end; but Jesus experienced all this. So he understands all that we are going through.

(2)   Humility

In this same verse we are told that he humbled himself. Although he was God, he also became fully human. Let us look at three features of this.

1. He humbled himself by not only leaving the splendour of heaven behind him but also belonging to a poor family. Joseph was just a carpenter, and Mary a simple young girl. They were not rich in this world's goods nor did they enjoy status. The wise men were surprised to find that the baby whose birth had been prophesied was not born in a palace!

2. He humbled himself by refusing to use his powers for his own ends. For instance, if he had thrown himself off the roof of the Temple and survived, he could have won a great following from the people he impressed by that, but these were not the kind of followers he was looking for.

3. He humbled himself by facing the shame of the Cross. Deuteronomy 21 pronounces a special curse on the man who is 'hung on a tree'; yet Jesus was willing to take that curse upon himself, as he knew this would be the means of our salvation.

Not many of us will suffer as much as Jesus did, but he was willing to do all this for his followers.

(3)   Obedience

Throughout his life on earth, Jesus walked in obedience to his Heavenly Father. Luke 2:51 tells us how he was obedient during his growing up. When he received baptism, the Father expressed approval of the life he lived (Luke 3:22). It was in obedience to his Father that Jesus set out on the road to Jerusalem, where he would be betrayed and executed (Luke 9:51). In Gethsemane he was able to pray "Father, if you are willing, take this cup from me; yet not my will but yours be done" (Luke 22:42).

Obeying his Heavenly Father became progressively difficult. How many of us would remain faithful and obedient if it meant intense pain and suffering? Yet, even in our own day, there are people who are ready to go through all this as a demonstration of their love for God. Jesus says in John 15:10: "If you keep my commands, you will remain in my love, just as I have kept my Father's commands and remain in his love". It is hard to imagine being ready to die for him, yet God is able to make even weak people such as ourselves prepared for this.

Even in Western society, it is not easy to keep God's commands, for there are so many distractions. Only Jesus, by his Spirit, can enable us to walk this way.

(4)   Death

The subject of 'death' is something that affects each one of us. Our age and experience may vary, but the one thing that is certain is that we are going to die. However, we know nothing of the time or the nature of our death. It is not unusual to reflect on this subject when you have reached old age, as I have.

Jesus, however, was a young man, probably 33 years old, when he died, and this took place in as cruel a way as can be imagined. He could have escaped, for he was all powerful; but, if he had chosen to do this, he would not have purchased our salvation. Only this most drastic of measures could bring us this gift.

So much space is given in the Bible to describing the death of Jesus and its purpose, because this is at the very centre of our Christian hope. He died in place of sinful man. In Galatians 3:13 we read: "Christ redeemed us from the curse of the law by becoming a curse for us" and Romans 5:8 reads: "But God demonstrates his own love for us in this: While we were still sinners, Christ died for us". If Jesus had not died in this way, there would be no Gospel.

So Christ died to atone for our sins; but there is a wider significance. We read in 1 Peter 2:21: "Christ suffered for you, leaving you an example". As Christians, we must be ready for the possibility of suffering. Unlike that of Christ, we shall not thereby purchase salvation for others, but, hopefully, they will be encouraged by our example, and given strength to remain loyal to God even if they also have to suffer because they can see how we are able to cope with it.

In another sense, we have died to the old way of life and begun a new Christ-filled life. In the 19th century a man called George Muller in Bristol founded an orphanage. Time and time again God provided for the needs of these poor orphans. When people asked him the secret of his success, he replied, "There was a time when George Muller died".

What privations have I suffered because of loyalty to God?

Chapter 14
THE EXALTATION OF JESUS
(2:9-11)

It is good to be present with a large group of Christians singing the praises of God. At such times we go beyond ourselves, and are taken up with the privilege of together ascribing to God the glory that is his.

We have taken a look at the life of Jesus on this earth and the way in which he humbled himself. The second half of this ancient Christian hymn goes on to declare the praises of Christ, who is now exalted in heaven. We too are called to look beyond the limitations of his life on earth to the glory that he now enjoys in the Father's presence.

Let us look at this in two stages.

(1)   Exalted by God

Verse 9 begins: "therefore". What follows is based on what has gone before. Paul is going to speak on how Jesus is exalted in heaven, but it is made clear that this is based on what he has previously been like. Yes, because Jesus is God, he deserves to be exalted; but in this instance it is linked with his obedience as a man. Despite all the temptations he faced, Jesus remained obedient, and his exaltation in heaven is the reward of that obedience. The problem with us as human beings is that, no matter how hard we try, we never find ourselves fully obedient in this life, and so any reward we get in heaven is basically God's gift to us rather than something we have deserved, whatever the standard of our accomplishment.

Next we read: "God exalted him to the highest place". As a result of his obedience, Jesus received this honour. There were two stages.

The first was his resurrection from the dead. Although he really died, he was raised to life again. According to 1 Corinthians 15:20,

Jesus in his resurrection has become "the first fruits of those who have fallen asleep". In other words, after our death, we who are believers will rise to enjoy new life. Now we can live lives full of hope because of what lies ahead of us.

The second was his ascension to heaven. His resurrection appearances were temporary only: his permanent home was in heaven. He had formerly been in heaven as God; but now he was there as man as well, in order to show that people who trust him will also one day like him enjoy a home in heaven. His presence in heaven is a demonstration that all true believers will also one day enjoy such an experience.

We are next told that he has been given a name that is above every other name. Sometimes human beings like to make a name for themselves. They like to think that others respect them because of who they are and what they have done. But whatever respect we may have for another human being, it pales into insignificance when compared with the name and character of Jesus himself. We may greatly respect the names of well known Christians, who have served God faithfully whilst on earth. Maybe we each have our own list of these 'heroes'. Jesus, however, goes well beyond that. His name is above all other names.

(2)   Worshipped by all beings

Now we turn from the picture of Jesus himself to the attitude of others toward him. This is described in verses 10 and 11.

At the name of Jesus every knee ought to bow. He is worthy to receive honour from every human being. The sad thing is that this does not happen. There are people who simply use his name as a swear word. There are others who respect him but only as a human teacher.

Three types of worshippers are described here. First there are those who worship in heaven. This must include the angels and Christians who have died and risen. From them he receives an undivided loyalty. Secondly, there are those who are still on earth. These are people who are still alive, but they have surrendered their lives to Christ, and therefore worship him despite human limitations. But this also includes a third group, namely those 'under the earth'. Here is a reference to the underworld. We may assume that this refers to those who have not previously acknowledged Jesus as Lord. Although they do not enjoy his salvation, they are in the end forced to admit his supremacy.

What is it that these beings confess? They confess that Jesus Christ is Lord. He is supreme, above every other being. When they acknowledge his supremacy, this also brings glory to God the Father.

All this could sound very cerebral. It describes such an exalted presence that it is hard to see how this impinges on everyday reality. Let me suggest four ways, then, in which these great truths may impact upon our daily lives.

First, it gives us a reason for assurance. In the Old Testament, when a Jew felt bogged down by his sin, it brought him some assurance to know that the High Priest was representing him in the Holy of Holies. Because of this, he could feel assured that God accepted him, despite his sin. But, with Jesus in our sights, the vision is much greater.

Secondly, it gives us reason for hope. All around us are people who do not care much about Jesus Christ. We who go to church are the exceptions; yet in many of our churches, the worship can seem dull, having no capacity to elevate our spirits. Yet our present imperfections will be a thing of the past when we discover a new quality of worship on our entry into heaven. The best is yet to be.

Thirdly, it gives us reason for praise. When we say "Jesus is Lord", we are pouring out our faith in such a statement. However, we still live in a world where so many people do not recognize his lordship. Those with sufficient insight can still see how Jesus is working in this troubled world; but for many people the negatives far outstrip the positives while we are still in this world.

Fourthly, it gives us reason for evangelism. Although at a human level, it is not always easy to see that Jesus is at work, with the eyes of faith we recognize his handiwork, and see this as a preparation for all that will be revealed in heaven. As we come to understand this more deeply for ourselves, we are all the more ready to share this precious truth with others, so that they too may become aware of the power of Jesus both in this world and the next.

What difference does it make to you to know that Jesus is in heaven?

Chapter 15
A HEALTHY FELLOWSHIP
(2:12-13)

After lifting our thoughts to heaven through that ancient Christian hymn, we now come down to earth again. Yet, as I studied the two verses that followed, I found I was very moved to observe what it says about our response to all this. In particular, this section speaks of three relationships which the Philippians all have as Christians and which we can also enjoy.

(1) Their Relationship with Paul

Paul goes on to say, "Therefore, my dear friends, as you have always obeyed – not only in my presence, but now much more in my absence...."

He has been speaking of Jesus' obedience to the Father. Now he goes on to speak of the obedience of Christians to himself. Paul is not putting on airs: to obey Paul, when he is faithful to God, is actually to obey the God who has sent him. When a leader is truly speaking up for God, there is something about his words which makes us feel we are listening to God himself. If he is just playing with his own ideas, then that is a different story.

This is all rather similar to family life when it is working properly. Children have to learn obedience to their parents, so that together they may enjoy a stable family life. Paul uses this analogy in 1 Thessalonians 2:11 where he says: "For you know that we dealt with each of you as a father deals with his own children". Paul looks to them for obedience not because he enjoys a sense of power, but because he represents God himself.

Two lessons follow from this. The first is that Christian leaders have responsibility for the growth of those who follow them. It is not just a matter of getting them converted: it is also a matter of giving them solid teaching, good pastoral care and an example of how to live. If those of us who exercise leadership are not fulfilling this role properly, we have no claim upon the loyalty of those who follow us. The second lesson is for new converts. Once enlightened, that is only the beginning of the story. They are in a sense children with much to learn, and their leaders can help them to grow in their knowledge and experience of God. That gradual process continues for the whole of the rest of our life on earth.

(2) Their Relationship with Each Other

The verse goes on: "continue to work out your salvation with fear and trembling". Our good works do not earn us salvation, but they show others that our salvation is real. If our faith does not result in good works, then others have a right to question its reality.

I believe that here Paul is not, however, speaking just of the individual's salvation but also of the spiritual health of the whole Christian community.

There is a book by Michael Wilson called "Health is for People". One thing he says in this book is: "Health is the milieu which enables people individually and socially to grow toward fullness of life". Do we see our own Christian fellowship as a place of growth?

Such spiritual progress does not just happen. Paul tells us that we have to work it out. In other words, we have to give regular visible expression to it.

Some people are put off the Christian faith altogether when they see church members bickering or criticizing one another. That is not what God intends for his people.

When, as a young National Serviceman, I joined a little group of people who behaved in this positive way, this led me to trust Jesus Christ as my Saviour.

If we want to make our own fellowship active in leading others to Christ, then we must do this with 'fear and trembling'.

So it is not a matter of good organization: it is rather about our subservience to God himself. As we humble ourselves before God, so we become effective instruments for outreach to others.

(3) Their Relationship with God

What we have looked at so far may seem hard to achieve. It is only possible as we maintain a close relationship with God. So the next verse reads: "for it is God who works in you to will and to act in order to fulfill his good purpose".

When my children were small and I sought to teach them to swim, it was not enough to stand on the side and encourage them. I had to get into the water with them and share their experience. So God is not helping us from some distant point, but he is right there with us. In fact, in the person of Jesus Christ he shared our normal human experience.

Now God works within us in order to fulfill his good purpose. Some people think that life has no meaning or purpose. But God has a special purpose for each one of us. If we want God to be working this out in our lives, what should be our attitude? I make two suggestions.

First we should want to follow it. We may meet up with other Christians and pray that together we may know the will of God. Or we may pray on our own to know his will. So either communally or singly we are seeking that God will work out his purposes through us. It is like the words of an old Christian hymn:

> *"Breathe on me, Breath of God,*
>
> *Until my heart is pure,*
>
> *Until with thee I will one will*
>
> *To do, or to endure."*

Secondly we need the power to follow it. It is a terrible thing to want to do something and yet to lack the power to carry it out. If God gives us the will to do something, then he can also give us the power to accomplish it. It is not a matter of seeking power for its own sake: many non-Christians do that. It is a matter of seeking power to do what God demands of us.

When Jesus in Gethsemane prayed "Not my will, however, but your will be done", an angel appeared from heaven to strengthen him. God's power was upon him, in all his human weakness, as he endured such punishment for our sakes. Nothing we have to do will be as hard as that, yet our power is from the same source.

God does not promise that we shall have easy lives; but he does promise to give us his power to enable us to do what is right.

Which relationships matter most to me?

Chapter 16
LIGHTS IN THE DARKNESS
(2:14-16a)

If you go into a dark room you can see little or nothing; but when you switch on the light, all this changes. God wants his people to be lights in a dark world.

Verse 15 speaks of a 'warped and crooked generation'. That is what people may be like who do not know God because of the power of sin in them. But, if we are Christians, we are meant to be light: our lives are a contrast to the lives of others around us and hopefully an inspiration to others. Paul gives us various examples of this.

(1) No Complaining

Verse 14 says: "Do everything without grumbling or arguing". A church fellowship is made up of those who know and love God, and the result of this should be a capacity to get on well with one another. But it does not always happen this way, for we each have our own personality. In 4:2, as we shall see later, Paul pleads with two women called Euodia and Syntyche, who have fallen out with one another. That is no uncommon thing, but such behaviour destroys the unity of a church fellowship.

However, we do not have to go simply to the Bible for instances of this. In our own church fellowship it is likely that there are people who do not get on with one another, and this can wreck the stability of the whole fellowship. Our differences should be made up if we want to have a positive effect on outsiders.

We are individual human beings, each with our own thoughts and attitudes. Others may not think the same way. Should we, then, strive to press our views on others? Or, rather, should we together come to God to seek his wisdom in this particular matter? That is the logical thing to do; and yet church fellowships have been brought into severe disunity just because people insist on their own way without testing their thoughts in the light of God's teaching or considering the viewpoint of others.

There is so much dissension in the outside world. In places this may have extremely damaging results. But we, since we are Christians, in our unity with one another, should be examples to the world outside.

(2) Blameless and Pure

Paul goes on to say that Christians should be blameless and pure. In this world, Christians are often criticized. They are sometimes criticized for attitudes and actions which are entirely imaginary. Christians accused on trumped up charges are subject to gross punishments. In such instances, the blame is with the attackers, not with them, yet they still have to suffer for it.

But we must examine our own lives, and make sure that we are not doing things which will enable others to criticize us with good reason.

The sad thing is that none of us is 100% pure. We all have our faults; but we should seek God's help in overcoming these, so that they may no longer be a hindrance when we are witnessing to others. The word 'pure' means 'unmixed'. It refers to metals which contain no alloy and wine that contains nothing that contaminates it. We may be tainted by our own wrongful thoughts and desires or by the example and allurement of others. But the closer we get to God, the purer that should make us. Like those presenting the old Jewish offerings, we should be able to offer ourselves to God without blemish or defect.

They are said to live in a warped and crooked generation. Although Paul was referring to a specific time and a specific society, we can apply such words, though with different examples, to other times and places. Those who do not know God, and who are living for themselves, are a long way from what God wants them to be. Moreover, they seek to persuade Christians to follow their own evil ways.

It was a sad day when the leader of the Liberal Democratic Party felt compelled to resign because his Christian views, especially regarding such matters as homosexual marriage and abortion, lost him much credibility amongst other members of his party. If we bravely follow God's standards in a society that is in moral decline, we likewise may face much opposition.

If people criticize us for our own perceived faults, we are in the wrong, and we must seek to correct our ways; but if they criticize us for our loyalty to God and his standards, then that is another matter entirely.

(3)   Shining Lights

We are to shine amongst others like stars in the sky. There is a great difference between a cloudy night, when nothing can be seen and a clear night, when the stars are visible in all their glory. Darkness in itself is not commendable, but when there are lights shining in the darkness all that is changed.

If there were no Christians in this world, it would indeed be a dark place, but when they are clearly demonstrating their faith the world is a much better place. We can make a difference as long as we hold firmly to the word of life. We are not trying to impress others by our good deeds. We simply seek to shine as God's people, living under the authority of his Word.

I heard many years ago about a tribe in Borneo that was largely made up of Christians. When any of them returned from visiting friends in another tribe, others did not ask, "Did you manage to put in a word for Christ?" Instead they would ask, "What did they say when you told them about Christ?" It was taken for granted that by word and example they would confront others with their Saviour. How natural is it for us to do this?

We must hold firmly to the word of life. If we begin to doubt God's word or to reinterpret it to suit our own interests, then we shall not have much effect on the lives of others. We may agree with them, but because of compromise rather than faithfulness. Such pacts are a sad travesty of what God really requires of us.

(4) Holding firmly

We are to hold firmly to the word of life. For us today, this represents Bible truth as it is read or preached. It is not a matter of merely receiving it in our intellect, but of taking it into our very being and holding on to it there.

The problem with a wet bar of soap is that it is too slippery: if we try to hold on to it, it may slip from our grasp. Some may see God's Word as hard to grasp. However, if we hold on to it by faith, it becomes something which we can indeed retain in our grasp. We must not be led astray by teaching that purports to be Christian, but which falls short of the set standards. Let us test what anyone teaches us in the light of the pure Word of God.

It is only as we hold on to God's Word that we are able to make good progress in the Christian life.

Am I bringing light into a dark place?

Chapter 17
THE EFFECT ON PAUL
(2:16b-18)

Paul is not just giving directions to the Philippians as to how they should live their Christian lives, He is also concerned to show how all this affects him personally; and, at the same time, he trusts that his own example will give them particular encouragement.

(1) Something to Boast About

Christian humility is a virtue. We are not out to make great names for ourselves. We are not out to boast about our success. And yet Paul does speak here about a kind of boasting.

This boasting is done not at the present time, however, but on the 'day of Christ'. It refers, of course, to the time of Christ's return. On that day it is Christ who will be pre-eminent. Anything we say then about ourselves and our work must be seen then in the light of this. The one who gets all the credit at that time will be not oneself but the Christ who has made all this possible.

Paul on that day will boast that he did not run or labour in vain. Sometimes, when a person exercises a spiritual ministry, it is not easy to see what effects it has had. Yes, there are some who can point to souls saved, to churches that have grown greatly and even to whole communities transformed; but for most of us the effects may not be clear to see.

As for myself, I have seen individual encouragements: for instance, young people whom I have helped toward faith have later entered the ministry of the Church. However, for the most part, whilst there have been small encouragements, there has been nothing dramatic. It was just a matter of trying to do my work faithfully.

One day I shall come before Jesus Christ, who has seen the whole picture. Although I have not had such dramatic success as St. Paul (nor the terrible suffering he sometimes experienced), I like to think that something of what I have done will have proved acceptable to my Lord and Saviour. And that is so for all of us. Jesus has seen what we have done, and he will show his approval of what we have accomplished when that great day comes. This should give us much encouragement in continuing to do all that we can.

(2)   Something Not Without Cost

Paul here speaks of himself being poured out like a drink offering. This was one of the rituals of pagan sacrifice. There is a comparison here between the pouring out of water or wine and that of human blood. So Paul is not just speaking here about the shedding of Jesus' blood at Calvary: he is also thinking of the cost to his followers; and for some that is also going to entail an ugly death.

For so many Christians these days this is an ongoing reality.

In my prayers I find myself concerned about situations that have arisen in many parts of the world. As I read about the suffering of Christians in Nigeria, North Korea, Syria, the Democratic Republic of Congo, Pakistan and other parts, it seems to me that those of us who have an easy, untroubled Christian life are in a distinct minority. If our continuance in the faith put us in danger of being martyred, would we still be so open about what we believe?

Although here in the west, we are unlikely to have to face such intense persecution, it is still true that there is a decline in Christian standards, and that those of us who maintain the old biblical standards may be thought odd, and may even be penalized for this. I was reading today about a man who was arrested because he was reading aloud from Scripture outside St. Paul's Cathedral. We are meant to 'go with the flow' and if we do not do this we may be criticized. This is particularly so with young people, who may be misunderstood by their peers.

If we belong to a Christ who was sacrificed for us, we must not think it strange if some sort of sacrifice creeps into our own lives as well.

But Paul is not just speaking of his personal sacrifice: those to whom he ministers must be prepared for sacrifice as well. Some will be arrested, even martyred, because of their loyalty to Christ. Paul is not bolstering them up with attractive promises, but speaking honestly about the cost involved in Christian service; and this is also a sharing in the cost which Jesus himself faced in dying to save us.

(3) Something to Produce Gladness

Some people are naturally happy. There is a character called Ginger in an Arnold Wesker play about National Servicemen. He has a problem: wherever he goes and whatever he does he has a grin on his face, and this annoys the drill instructor who is trying to make him conform to what is considered normal. Some of us have a more cheerful attitude than others. However, the gladness spoken of here is not a natural affinity: it is something which comes from our faith in God.

It may be a gladness which has no relation to external circumstances. We see it on the faces of people who are being persecuted for their faith. How can they look happy when they are being so badly treated? It makes us wonder how we would behave if we were in such circumstances.

But it can also be a gladness which comes from observing what is going on around us. So Paul is glad because of the good news he hears of the Philippian Christians. That they are faithfully following God, whatever the pressures, brings great gladness to Paul. Whenever we see our fellow Christians holding on to their faith, this should bring us much joy.

However, it is not just a gladness which we enjoy alone. Here Paul bids the Philippian Christians to be glad and rejoice with him.

Christian joy is something to be shared with our fellow Christians. We hear of Christians weeping together (and there is a place for that too) but it is also good to see Christians rejoicing together in God.

We may find it hard to rejoice even under our normal circumstances; but Paul is able to rejoice even when he is in prison, for that joy comes from God; and he wants his fellow Christians to share in this great experience.

Do you feel close enough to others to share these deep emotions with them?

Chapter 18
ABOUT TIMOTHY
(2:19-24)

Paul has already said a lot about Jesus and about himself. Now he begins to talk about his two colleagues, Timothy and Epaphroditus, who merit a chapter each in this book.

He has one main reason for sending Timothy all the way to Philippi: he wants to be encouraged by news of how the Christians there are faring. Not only does he plan to send Timothy to them; but he also hopes that, after his hoped for release, he can visit Philippi himself.

Now let us take a look at what he says about young Timothy.

(1)   His Background

He has served Paul as a son might serve his father. As for his real family, although Paul does not speak of it here, we know from other places what the details are. His mother was a Jewess and his father was a Greek. It seems that his mother's influence was stronger than his father's. So we read in 2 Timothy 3:15 that ever since he was a child he had received instruction in the Holy Scriptures, even though he had not received circumcision. In 2 Timothy 1:5 we learn that his grandmother Lois and his mother Eunice had both given him a lot of encouragement as Jewish Christians. We do not know exactly how he came to faith, but he could well have been one of Paul's converts on that first visit. Probably the teaching he received from his family was ample preparation for this.

Although there are people who suddenly become Christians without any preparation, there are many others who need a long period of preparation before they make that step of faith. The evangelist who appears on the scene is simply, under God's hand, completing what others have begun.

Of course, we are not Christians simply because we come from a Christian family: each of us has to make his or her own decision to follow Jesus.

For Timothy, his conversion was only the beginning: a long period of spiritual growth ensued. We read in Acts 16:2, at a time when Paul returned to Lystra, that all people spoke well of the young man. Recognizing this, Paul suggested taking him with him on his missionary journeys. Paul circumcised him so as to make him more acceptable to the Jewish communities, and they set off.

So we see that it was Paul who guided Timothy into undertaking Christian work. It is good when a spiritual leader perceives that God is calling someone into full time service. It is also good when a young convert takes that initiative, but is also assessed by those with more experience. In either case, it is not a matter of a young Christian doing everything on his own initiative.

The path would not be smooth. There was a time when Timothy gave up in the middle of a missionary journey and went back home. After this, Paul found it hard to accept Timothy for quite some time, but by the time he writes this letter the ruction is over, and he knows he can trust his young friend. Even a mature Christian leader like Paul was for a while unable to perceive the real potential of this young convert.

(2) His Character

But let us look more deeply at the character of this man, especially with reference to the language with which Paul here describes him. There are two ways in which he shares in the work and the burdens of Paul.

Firstly, he shares the same concern. Paul says in v.20: "I have no one else like him, who will show genuine concern for your welfare". We have already seen in Chapter 1 how Paul himself prays for them and thanks God for them, how he holds them in his heart, and how his feelings for them come from the heart of Christ himself. Paul has the heart of a true pastor; but now he perceives that same heart in young Timothy.

It is all too easy to get concerned with the administration of a church, with running programmes, with keeping the site clean and so on. These things are important, but even more important than these things is God's work in the hearts and lives of individuals. The Church is not just an organization but a community of people.

It is also too easy to lack concern about the growth of others because we are simply taken up by our own affairs. This mistake is outlined in the next verse, where we read: "For everyone looks out for their own interests, not those of Jesus Christ". Yes, it is still important to take note of our own spiritual progress and to seek to grow nearer to the Lord, but we must not do this at the expense of our care for others. Jesus is concerned for the whole Church, and we should share that concern. This also goes beyond out local congregation. What about those countries where the Church is under severe persecution? Are we concerned for the Christians there?

Secondly he shares in the same service. In verse 22 we read: "But you know that Timothy has proved himself, because as a son with his father he has served with me in the work of the Gospel". For Timothy it is not all talk: his relationship with Paul and with God himself leads him to action.

Because it was Paul who led Timothy to Christ, they now enjoy a relationship which resembles that of father and son. Timothy recognizes Paul's authority, and works with him in consciousness of that relationship. Both of them are deeply concerned for the Gospel and its effect on other people's lives.

Whilst we are very grateful for those who have helped us in the Christian life, we rejoice that we are partners with them in reaching out to others.

For the time being, Paul is in prison and thus unable to visit the converts. Timothy, however, is under no such restrictions, so he is able to deputize for Paul in his missionary travels. When it is a bit clearer what is going to happen to him, he will send Timothy back to the local church, bringing the latest news about himself to those who are concerned for him. Because they respect Paul, the people will respect Timothy also. But, hopefully, this is only for a time, and Paul will be released and in a position to visit them in person once more. It all depends on how the Lord works things out.

It is good for us also to remember those who have helped us much in our Christian lives and to seek to live the sort of life they would wish for us.

How do we relate to our spiritual leaders?

Chapter 19
ABOUT EPAPHRODITUS
(2:25-30)

When I was leaving my first curacy, my vicar gave a speech in which he said I was like Epaphroditus. However, when I take a look at this man, I feel that I fall a long way short.

His name means 'comely' or 'charming'. He came from Philippi, but, like Timothy, he had been sent to Rome to minister to Paul in his imprisonment. Now Paul is sending him back again with this letter.

Let us look at his relationship with Paul and his attitude to himself.

(1) His Relationship with Paul

There are four words used here which describe that relationship.

First he is called '*my brother*'. Of course, he was not related physically to Paul, but their relationship was so special that Paul regarded him spiritually as his brother. In the same way, we can call our fellow Christians our brothers and sisters.

Secondly he is described as '*co-worker*'. He is engaged in the same task as Paul – that of bringing the Gospel to others. The Church in Philippi began when Paul was on his second missionary journey. At that time Lydia and others became the first converts. Maybe Epaphroditus was among them. He was not only converted, but he wanted to share his faith with others. In that sense he became Paul's co-worker. I remember that less than a year after my own conversion I worked on a beach mission in North Wales, and this meant I had a special relationship with others who were taking part in that work. We were all involved in the same task.

Thirdly he is described as 'fellow-soldier'. I remember, as a missionary on furlough, going one time to worship at my home church in Blackpool. The church was packed with elderly people

81

whom I did not know. I discovered that they were taking part in a reunion of the 3rd, 4th and 7th Tank Regiments, who had fought in the Second World War. Fighting against a common foe had enabled them to establish a clear bonding with one an other. We as Christians fight for God against a common enemy. It is not a historical battle, but one which we continue to fight while we remain on this earth.

Fourthly he is described as a '*messenger*'. I can remember as a teenager taking part in a Shakespearean play. However, it was not very demanding, for I was simply a messenger, reading from a script. Here a messenger, like an apostle, is sent out with the authority of the sender. He is to speak not his own words but the words of the sender. But in this instance there is something more. Epaphroditus has been sent by the Philippian Church to Rome to minister to Paul's needs. He is to give to Paul all the help which they would have given if they had been able to go there personally. So when Paul looks at the light in this one man's eyes as he serves him, he sees, as it were, the light in the eyes of the whole congregation from which he comes.

(2) His Personal Situation

Although this is just a short passage, we still learn six things about this man.

First he sacrificed his personal prospects. He might have had a good job, found himself a wife, and enjoyed local perks, but when he was asked by the local Christians to go to Rome to minister to Paul's needs, he agreed to go. There is no indication of the personal cost and the length of time he would be away, but he was happy to be the Church's messenger. How many of us are happy to go where God, through his Church, sends us, rather than simply enjoying our personal prospects? Of course, the happiest state is when the two coincide.

Secondly, he longs for his friends back home. He is quite a distance away from them and does not know how they are faring. But it is not a case of 'out of sight, out of mind'. Wherever he is, he continues to hold them in his heart.

Going to a faraway place can, however, be a lonely business. For me it was hard to leave home and go all the way to Taiwan as a missionary. But God was still with me, and I was amongst new friends, so that the whole experience became very positive. I did not have the benefit of immediate internet access with friends which people enjoy today, but, then, neither did Epaphroditus.

Thirdly, he has been ill. We do not know what the illness was, but we do know that word of his illness had got back to Philippi. It was not a light illness, for he almost died.

Rather than complaining about the personal effects of this illness, he was sad because of the distress this news causes his friends back home. As Christians we are not protected from illness, but we have the assurance that God is still with us even when circumstances are negative.

Fourthly, he was kept from death. This healing was a product of God's mercy, so he was thankful to God. But there was more: healing not only brought comfort to Epaphroditus himself, but it also spared Paul further suffering. Sometimes Christians when they fall ill do not recover; but they can take comfort from the fact that Jesus is still with them.

Fifthly, he was recovered enough to make the long journey back to Rome. His appearance would give the other Christians joy on two accounts: first they would be glad to see that Epaphroditus had recovered from his illness, and they would also be pleased to have up to date news about Paul himself.

Sixthly, he was to be received with joy. Indeed, Paul hoped his fellow Christians would honour him, for he had almost lost his life for Christ's sake. He had risked his life to do what the others could not do – make a long and arduous trip and minister for a period of time to Paul's own needs. So he obeyed God by going to minister to Paul, and he obeyed God by returning to the local Church and giving them up to date news.

There are people like Epaphroditus who may not appear to have accomplished great things, but God is pleased with them, for they have ministered to others despite the cost.

Am I ready to go anywhere God sends me without feeling a sense of loss?

Chapter 20
EXTERNAL AND TRUE RELIGION
(3:1-3)

Paul now bids the Philippians to rejoice in the Lord. Being imprisoned for the faith was not a happy situation to be in, yet Paul was still able to rejoice. That was because his joy was not dependent on outward circumstances, but on the Lord in whom he had placed his trust.

In view of the fact that he has already spoken about rejoicing, Paul might be accused of repetition. But it is not mere repetition: sometimes saying something more than once is the only way to get important truths across to the hearers.

There is a story of a man who went to hear George Whitefield preach. The great man preached on the text "Ye must be born again". He went to hear him on a second occasion and the text was the same. When this happened for a third time, he went up to the preacher and asked why his messages were so repetitive. Whitefield looked him straight in the eye and said, "Because you must be born again".

It is also said of Juan Carlos Ortiz, ministering in Argentina, that he would teach a doctrine persistently until he felt the hearers had got hold of it, and only then would he move on to something else.

So Paul is not afraid to repeat himself. This is very different from having nothing new to say! It is when we have truly grasped an important lesson that we are ready to go on to something different.

Now he goes on to speak of false teachers. Often when the truth is preached, others will come along to distort what has been said. Paul is very much aware of this, and so he goes on to warn his hearers about this. In so doing he makes a comparison between a mere external religion and true religion.

(1) External Religion

Paul describes these false teachers in not very flattering terms. Let us look at the three words he uses.

First they are described as *dogs*. We live in a society where people keep dogs as pets. They are seen as friendly and cooperative, and there is a tendency to give in to their demands. To the Jews of that time, however, a dog would be seen as a despised and unclean creature. The dogs described here are not household pets, but wild creatures, relying on their wits for survival. When people are like dogs they are ready to do anything to further their own selfish cause. This is rather an extreme way of describing them, but Paul wants to make it clear that their position is completely untenable.

Secondly they are described as *evildoers*. This word is less open to misinterpretation. They rely on their works for salvation without really understanding the taint of sin upon them. They are described a mutilators of the flesh – that is, they think that, because they are circumcised, they are acceptable to God, quite apart from the poor morality which they practise. It is only too easy today for church people to rely on externals for their salvation. But it is possible to have all the outwards trappings of religion without enjoying the real thing. If we have the external trappings but we do not love and follow Christ, what hope have we?

Thirdly they are described as *mutilators of the flesh*. This is a reference to circumcision, and this is something which the Jews have been told they must do to their male children. But it is not the external marks but the regular practice of good morality which is pleasing to God. That good morality is itself not an attempt to earn salvation but a proof that we have already found it. If we are merely relying on externals such as our baptism and confirmation for our acceptance with God, we are making a grave mistake.

(2)   True Religion

We have taken a look at the negative side. What about the positive side? What kind of people does God want us to be?

Here we are told that we are the true circumcision. That is, we are not relying on externals for our acceptance with God, but we are those in whom God is doing a new work. Circumcision was used to make a person into a real Jew. In Colossians baptism is described as a new kind of circumcision. When a person is baptized as an indication that he has faith in Jesus, this is a whole new beginning. Of course, a person may undergo the outward ceremonies without being changed inside, in which case this serves no useful purpose.

So if we have undergone the 'true circumcision' how should this show in our lives? There are three effects mentioned here.

First we serve God by the Spirit. Now it is possible to go to formal services, to go through the rituals and yet to gain nothing from them. It is also possible to perform acts of Christian service without truly relating to God. It is not a matter of what we do outwardly, but of our inner dependence on the Holy Spirit. We all received the Spirit when we put our trust in Jesus, but many of us fail to appreciate its significance; and there may be need to come to Jesus once again not for our salvation but for a filling with the Spirit, thus energizing us for our Christian life and work. We then go on to depend on the Spirit daily in all that we do.

Secondly we boast in Christ Jesus. It is only too easy to boast about the Christian service we think we have performed; but we would not be able to do any of this if it were not for the presence of Jesus Christ in our lives. We boast then in who Jesus is and what he has done for us; only then can we trust him to enable us do work that is truly acceptable.

Thirdly we put no confidence in the flesh. Here 'the flesh' means accomplishing things simply through our human abilities. If we are to perform lasting work for Christ it must be the vision of Christ and the strength drawn from him that enable us, not our own human abilities.

There are people in history like John Wesley, who was so keen to serve God rightly that he even went all the way to North America to spread the Gospel; but all that he did there was 'of the flesh'. It was only when he had a new experience of God and relied entirely on him for power that he became a true vehicle for God. Nowadays we can read all about his extensive ministry which resulted from that transformation.

Yes, it is only too possible to try and serve God without relying on the God-given power which we need to make our work effective.

On what do you rely for results in your Christian service?

Chapter 21
A CHANGE OF ATTITUDE
(3:4-9)

Has there been a time in your life when everything changed and suddenly you had a whole new way of looking at things?. When Paul had his vision of Christ on the road to Damascus, that was when everything changed for him. True conversion to Christ changes our life for ever. Let us look at what he was like before and after the experience.

(1) Paul's Former Experience

He was always a religious man. In the earlier part of his life, however, it was the Jewish faith which dominated, and for him it was a matter of following external laws rather than having an internal relationship with God. More than this, he severely persecuted those who proclaimed a Christian message. It was just like the way in which Paul described his fellow Jews in Romans 10:2: "they are zealous for God, but their zeal is not based on knowledge". Here we find seven features of his old life, which gave him a mistaken confidence concerning his relationship with God.

1. He was circumcised when he was a week old. He had no choice in the matter. His parents arranged for him to have this operation so that, externally at least, he would look like a Jew. In our own day, though less often than previously, many people are baptized as babies as a formality, but this is no guarantee that they will grow up as believers. I am glad that I was baptised when I was very small. As a result of this, I went to a church school and eventually went forward for Confirmation. But God still had to do a new work.

2. He belonged to the people of Israel. His parents bore the external mark of being Jewish, so they wanted their son to be the same.

For Paul, though, it was not just a legacy: it was something so important to him that he would staunchly oppose anyone who had a different view.

3. He belonged to the tribe of Benjamin. He could trace his history back to that son whom his father David greatly favoured. This was the tribe which gave the first king to Israel, and it was the one tribe which remained loyal afterwards to David and his successors. We may be able to look back to such ancestors, but this does not win us our own personal salvation.

4. He was a Hebrew of the Hebrews. That is, he was not of mixed race but was the genuine article. He had been brought up to speak Hebrew, the mother tongue. But it is all too easy to use religious language without having a true commitment to God. This can also happen among church people.

5. In regard to the Law he was a Pharisee. These men were marked out by their great loyalty to the written Law. Unfortunately, however, over the years they had added to it and it had become a legalistic system that was far removed from what Moses had given. It was all about externals rather than being an internal religion. It is only too easy for us also to be governed by externals rather than having a living faith.

6. He was a persecutor of the Church. Thinking that these 'Christians' were misguided, he did all he could to get them arrested in order to minimize their influence. All this he did out of supposed loyalty to God. For him this was not a minor issue, for he travelled far and wide in order to arrest these men, whom he considered to be enemies to the true faith. Ironically, it was during one of these journeys that he was converted to the true faith.

7. His righteousness was based on the external law. He thought that by keeping religiously to the external demands of the Law he was currying favour with God. What he did not then understand was that a God-given faith was much more important than merely seeking to adhere to external regulations. He was unaware of the fact that, no matter how zealous he was in his keeping of the Law, he still fell far short of God's requirements.

So this was a picture of Paul as he used to be. He was always very zealous for God, but in those early days his zeal was based on externals rather than on the truth as it was in Jesus.

It was his experience on the Damascus road which changed all this. It was on that occasion that he met with Christ face to face, and became temporarily blind; but when in due course his physical eyes were opened, it was also an indication that he now had new spiritual eyes.

We thus have a duty to examine ourselves. Are we relying merely on external rituals and customs to give us a relationship with God, or have we come into a wholly new personal relationship with him?

The whole of the Old Testament is the story of the Jewish people – how God called them to himself and time and time again acted on their behalf when they were in difficulty. But we now have the New Testament as well. The word 'testament' is the same as the word 'covenant'. We are brought into a new relationship with God that is based not on anything we earn by our external works but on what God has done through Jesus Christ, notably his death for our sins and his rising on the third day.

Christianity is all about God's grace; but even so we may forget this, and still try to earn our salvation by the things that we do. If so, we are placing ourselves alongside the pre-conversion Paul and that will not bring us into salvation. Like Paul, we need to be changed.

How far do you resemble Paul in your thinking?

Chapter 22
WHAT HAS CHANGED?
(3:7-9)

In the past Paul relied on all the externals of Jewish religion; but after meeting Jesus he was a changed man. He goes on to describe what has changed.

(1) Profit and Loss

First he speaks of profit and loss: "But whatever were gains to me I now consider loss for the sake of Christ". As a child I used to think that God had a big pair of scales into which he put our good and our bad deeds, and woe betide us if it were to come down on the wrong side. But if we are relying on anything we have done for salvation it does not work that way. God has a new way of measuring. It is the whole distinction between law and grace. If we are relying simply on our own feeble attempts to keep God's Law, we have no grounds for hope.

(2) Loss and Gain

Secondly he speaks of loss and gain. The precise words are: "What is more, I consider everything a loss because of the surpassing worth of knowing Christ Jesus my Lord". He has already spoken of loss and repeats that; but he also stresses what he has gained, and that is a knowledge of Jesus Christ. What is the point of living a life of good works if we ignore the one from whom all goodness comes? If we simply rely on our good works for salvation, then we have no confidence, for we may do terrible things that will give us no hope any more of acceptance by God. So if we are honest about our behaviour, this can never inspire in us a true confidence.

(3) Garbage

Thirdly he speaks of garbage. While I was writing this, a council truck came to empty the black bins. At other times, trucks will come to empty the brown and blue bins. We are given careful instructions as to what should go in each bin, but it is a complicated process. But all our supposed good works are like garbage if we think of them as a means of salvation. Paul puts it this way: "for whose sake I have lost all things. I consider them garbage, that I may gain Christ and be found in him". What is the point of merely accumulating piles of rubbish? God's standards are so high, that we can never expect to adhere to them simply by our own efforts.

As a man of 81, I am blessed with plenty of this world's goods. I have good furniture, lots of books, television and music players, kitchen implements, a piano, many paintings and so on. When I die I will not be able to take anything with me. What to do with these things will be a problem for my two sons. In a sense, precious as these things are, many of them will at that time simply be seen as garbage, for the life that has embraced them will have been snuffed out. Shall we, then, place all our emphasis on this world's goods, or can we see beyond them?

(4) True Righteousness

Fourthly he speaks of true righteousness. He says: "and be found in him, not having a righteousness of my own that comes from the law, but that which is through faith in Christ – the righteousness that comes from God on the basis of faith. True righteousness, therefore, is not earned, but bestowed on us in response to our faith.

Each reader of this chapter (assuming there are some) has his or her own individual way of life; but the one thing we share with other Christians is that we find ourselves accepted by God not on the basis of what we have done, but in whom we have placed our faith.

I was baptised as a newly born child, during a family service – an event of which, of course, I have no recollection. I attended a church school. When I was at secondary school I was confirmed along with other pupils at the church near the school. After this I began to attend my local church regularly. On two occasions clergy asked to speak with me, and encouraged me to consider entering the ministry of the Church. But, looking back, I do not consider I was a real Christian at the time.

This came when I was doing National Service and I was posted to Ballykelly in Northern Ireland. There I met a group of airmen who took their faith very seriously. I discovered that they had each had a conversion experience. After a period of seeking, I also took Jesus Christ as my Saviour; and now I look back to that as the start of my real Christian life. My 'Damascus Road' happened to be in Northern Ireland. It feels strange now that my home in retirement is also in that part of the world.

When I come before God's judgment seat, God will not weigh my good and bad deeds and decide whether the one side is weightier than the other: his judgment of me will simply be taken from what Jesus accomplished when he died on the Cross for my sins.

My response has simply been to put my faith in Christ. I have trusted him for my salvation; and through his working in my life I have been able to do things that would have been beyond my mere human power.

So God will not put my good works in one scale and my bad ones in the other and make a comparison. That is not the meaning of grace. Nevertheless, if I have chosen to live by faith in Christ and to live under God's grace, this should have made a difference to the way I behave. I do good works not in order to gain merit but in order to thank God for what he has already done for me in Christ.

Are you relying on 'good works' for salvation or something else?

Chapter 23
PAUL'S GOALS
(3:10,11)

When you become a Christian, you have, in a sense 'arrived'. But in another sense that is only the start. You have a long life ahead of you of walking with God until the day comes when he takes you to be with himself. It would be folly to imagine that, now that you have become a Christian, there are no more goals to aim for. In a sense, our conversion is only the beginning.

To Paul, then, conversion is not the end of the road but the beginning of a new road. He has a whole set of new aims which are described here. In particular there are three aims.

(1) To Know Christ and the Power of his Resurrection

Paul wants to know Christ. But surely since that experience on the road to Damascus, he has already got to know him. Yes, he has, but there is so much room for that knowledge to develop.

I thought I knew my wife on the day of our marriage; but that was just the start of an ongoing period of growth in our relationship. If that is true for us at a human level, it is all the more true on a spiritual level.

He speaks here of knowing the power of his resurrection. The resurrection of Jesus Christ from the dead was a unique event. There is no parallel to this in the rest of history. It was an event that came from the power of God. In Ephesians 2:19-20 Paul speaks of "his incomparably great power for us who believe". He goes on to say, "That power is the same as the mighty strength he exerted when he raised Christ from the dead and seated him at his right hand in the heavenly realms". The same power, then, which raised Christ from the dead, now works in us to accomplish God's purposes in our lives.

95

It is not a matter just of personal striving. If this verse were more real to us, how could we contemplate any kind of sin?

In Romans 6:4-5 we read: "We were therefore buried with him through baptism into death in order that, just as Christ was raised from the dead through the glory of the Father, we too may live a new life. For if we have been united with him in a death like his, we will certainly also be united with him in a resurrection like his." Thus do we share the victory of Christ.

So to be a Christian is not just to enjoy the legal verdict of 'not guilty', it is to be united with Christ. Being a Christian is not something merely formal, it is a matter of relating to Christ in everything. We need to apply the power of Christ's resurrection to each and every situation in which we find ourselves.

(2)   To Share in his Sufferings and become Like him in his Death

God never promises us that, as Christians, we shall be free from suffering. There are sufferings which we share with other people, and there are those which come upon us because of our loyalty to Christ.

There are people who refer to illness, bereavement and other misfortunes as crosses to be borne; but it is suffering because of our loyalty to Christ which is chiefly being spoken of here.

Paul knew a lot about this kind of suffering. He says in 2 Corinthians 4:8-10: "We are hard pressed on every side, but not crushed; perplexed, but not in despair; persecuted, but not abandoned; struck down, but not destroyed. We always carry around in our body the death of Jesus, so that the life of Jesus may also be revealed in our body."

We may not suffer as much as Paul did because of our faith, but the principle is the same. There are troubles that come upon us because of our loyalty to Christ. We may be criticized for our supposedly narrow viewpoints, we may be excluded from more liberal groupings, we may risk losing our job and so on. But this is mild treatment compared with the way many Christians are treated because of their faith in countries where Islam, Hinduism and even Buddhism are predominant. Then there are countries like Mainland China where Communism prevails. In such places loyalty to Christ may even result in death. Who then are we to complain of our own lot?

Christ was willing to face death out of loyalty to his Heavenly Father. Can we complain, then, about any suffering that we may have?

For the saints in biblical times there was not only suffering, but joy in the midst of it. The great Methodist preacher, George Whitefield, once wrote: "I believe the saints of old never had so much comfort as when they were obliged to shut the doors for fear of the Jews and to hide themselves in dens and caves of the earth. The Lord prepare us all for such an hour."

(3)   To Attain the Resurrection of the Dead

The first two goals referred to our present lives, but this one refers to the life beyond.

Buddhists are looking for Nirvana – a state in which they cast off all emotions, good and bad. The Existentialists, though seeking to authenticate their present existence, face an anticipated oblivion in the future. Others have varied views concerning the future, but it is usually associated only with this life. The Christian, however, is looking forward to a life beyond this one in which everything is far better than before.

Paul here incorporates the word 'somehow'. This does not mean that he has doubts about attaining the resurrection. It just means that we do not know what the ongoing process will be like. Some may suffer a violent death, others may die more peacefully; but what matters is the new life that follows.

In this life all is not complete. We are full of uncertainties concerning life conditions and the nature and time of our death; but one day all that will be behind us as we enter into that fullness which God has prepared for us. In old age I am blessed with excellent health. Thus I have a lot for which to thank God. But I do not know what lies ahead. It may be that I will have to face a time of sickness that is hard to bear. The truth is I simply do not know. It is the thought of what God has prepared for us after this earthly life is over which enables us to face our current limitations and dangers with confidence.

What are we looking forward to?

Chapter 24
PAUL'S PROGRESS
(3:12-14)

Paul has been speaking about his goals. If you are playing a game such as soccer, it is the goals that count. However well or badly a team has played, it will be judged by the number of goals scored. Nevertheless there is much more to a game of soccer than goal scoring. Each player has a part to play; there will be a variety of moves, some good, some bad. But it is in the context of the whole game and the way it is played that the goal scoring takes place.

Whilst Paul has his eyes on the goal, he is also concerned for the whole state of the game. Here in these verses we see more of this.

(1)   There is Still a Long Way to Go

It is one thing to press toward the goal; but the process is a long one. Paul has to work hard in many ways to prepare himself for the achieving of the goal.

It is not that Paul doubts his entry one day into heaven; but that remains in the future and there is still a lot of work he needs to do to prepare for this. The one thing he is sure of is that Jesus Christ has taken hold of him. His future in heaven is in no doubt because Jesus is to be trusted. But he is not there yet, and there is still plenty to be done.

Jesus saved him not in order that he should just put his feet up and wait for the goal to be achieved. Jesus has a purpose for his life on earth, and it is for him to be aware of that purpose and to work things out in practice. It does not mean that his life (or ours) will be easy: there could be many demands, but the outcome is assured. Our 'sanctification' is a way of preparing us for heaven.

The verse Hebrews 2:10 also speaks into this situation: "In bringing many sons and daughters to glory, it was fitting that God, for

99

whom and through whom everything exists, should make the pioneer of their salvation perfect through what he suffered". If we have to suffer, Jesus suffered much more, but it was all in order to prepare us for entry into heaven.

(2) Just Keep the Goal in Mind

When you decide to run a marathon, it is not simply something you take in your stride. There is need for months of training to build up your stamina; and even on the day itself a lot of effort is needed. There may be times, especially when you are in the closing stages, when you feel like giving up, but you press on because you have the goal before you. In a drawer I have six medals, all awarded at the close of the marathons I ran.

The goal that lies before us is our new life in heaven with God; but that is not something that we just drift towards. It requires a lot of effort. We must take pains to lead a good Christian life, not in order to earn a place in heaven, but to prove that the God who is working in us here and now has also prepared a place for us there. God does not promise us an easy life; but he does promise us his strength so that we do not give up.

I used to find that, in the closing yards of a race, I managed to go a little faster: even though I was tired, the sight of the goal spurred me on to greater effort. We tend to think of old age as a time of slowing down; but it feels good when, even in advanced years, we are capable of extra effort in preparation for achieving the goal. The race is not over until we get past the finishing line.

(3) Have a Right Attitude to the Past

Paul has spoken of looking forward. But what about the past? What should be the right attitude to that? If we are running a race and we keep looking back, it may slow us down. We may learn from the past, but we are now straining forward to the future. Paul may have thought of his life before conversion; he may have thought of God's hand on his ministry up to that point. One can learn from these past experiences, but progress is made only as we move forward. We must not be like Lot's wife who, just when deliverance was coming, spoiled it all by looking back.

There is a story of a woman who had had a 'blessed experience'. This was all recorded on a piece of paper which she stored in the attic. Every now and again she would pull out this 'blessed experience'; to share with others; but one day she found it had been eaten by moths and there was nothing left to show to others!

Whilst he is thankful for the past, Paul presses on toward the goal. He wants to live in such a way that he enjoys God's approval of what he achieves, and only then will he be ready to enter into all that God has prepared for him in the next life.

(4)   Keep Pressing On

The BBC loves to show old episodes of 'Dad's Army'. The youngest member of the Home Guard in Warmington-on-Sea is sometimes reprimanded for sucking his thumb. He is supposed to be a soldier, yet he is reduced to childish habits.

Our Christian life is a time of growth, of maturing. Paul likes to think that he is mature, and that many of those with whom he has fellowship have also reached a period of maturity. This does not mean that the goal has been achieved, but he is well on course. Sadly, Christians are not always in agreement with one another. If we differ from other Christians in our thinking, let us not dismiss one another but believe that God can work it all out. The worst thing is that this should divide us from other Christians.

Paul here claims to be mature, but he makes no claim to be perfect. However much we may have grown in the Christian life, there is still room for improvement. He hopes that others who consider themselves to be mature will still, with him, press on toward the goal. At the very least, they should live up to what they have already attained. Nobody should go backwards.

What are your goals right now?

Chapter 25
CHRISTIAN MATURITY
(3:14-16)

We are all at different stages in our Christian walk. Some are new Christians, and so many things have an air of novelty. Some have been Christians for a long time. Or maybe some who read this do not feel they are yet real Christians.

Paul has been writing about his own Christian experience; but now suddenly he turns to face his fellow Christians and to challenge them.

Here there are three topics to engross us.

(1)   Dealing With the Future

As I have said, we are all at different stages of our Christian experience. Nobody can say that he has 'arrived'. That is something which must wait until we get into the next world.

Paul has been writing from his own mature point of view. He has shown how he has turned away from his former immature self and grown a lot. He is also straining towards the goal that awaits him when he reaches heaven.

For the time being, however, he is to live not in the past or in the future but in the present.

It would be only too easy to treat Christian doctrine as something purely intellectual. But for Paul, grasping Christian truth is to make a profound impact on the way we behave here and now.

He is here addressing those who would call themselves mature. It is interesting to take a look at our own lives. As I have indicated, I became a true Christian while doing National Service. This was followed by three years as a student at Cambridge, where I was privileged to receive Christian teaching from prominent leaders with a real gift for preaching. By the time I graduated, therefore, I had a good understanding of the Christian faith. I went on to study more at theological college, so that when I entered the ordained ministry I could feel even more mature.

And yet, in a sense, I was not mature. Despite my privileges, I still had a lot to learn. Through the rest of my life I have continued to learn, and I am still learning. It is a sign of maturity that I recognize my true maturity still lies ahead, when God will take me into a wholly different world.

It is good that we continue to grow in the Christian life and we must never assume that we have now got it all! Whoever we are, we still have a lot to learn.

(2)   Handling Differences

But we are not all the same. We are all at different levels of maturity. Because of this, we may see the same thing with different eyes.

This could be dangerous. It could mean that disunity is bred among a Christian flock.

Of course, we are not meant to be carbon copies of one another. Life would be very boring if we were all exactly the same. Even when we are studying the scriptures together, we may differ in our interpretation. As long as we do not differ on basic and essential doctrines, there is nothing wrong with this. We may even be able to help one another as we look at certain matters from different points of view.

It is important, though, that we do not remain so convinced of our own viewpoint that we are deaf to other suggestions. The suggestion is made here that, if Christians see a matter with different eyes, God will show us what is the truth. So we must never look at matters simply from our point of view, but look to God to show us the truth and help us to walk in it.

Satan loves to divide the Church. That is one reason that there are so many denominations. It is not that one denomination has everything right and the others are wrong. Often we differ merely in externals, and we can thus live together peaceably. Even when the differences involve bigger subjects, such as our attitude to the Holy Spirit, it is still possible to be united on most points and even to treat those with a different viewpoint as brothers and sisters in the Lord. All the time, we must also be open to the possibility that God will change our own way of thinking on some issues.

(3)   Taking our Stand

I can well remember that address toward the end of my university days. Here we were, all keen members of the Christian Union; but the speaker said that some of us would fall away. We felt like the disciples at the Last Supper. Surely we could never conceive anything like that happening to us! Yet there was a sad truth about his words. Whilst many of us would rejoice in a keen Christian life throughout the ensuing decades of growth, others would unexpectedly turn away from the truth they had embraced.

So Paul here speaks of living up to what we have already attained. It is by God's help that we have reached the level of maturity that we currently embrace. We must not imagine, however, that we shall always maintain that same level of maturity. Some of us may decline, but God's desire is that we may all continue to grow.

We must live up to what we have attained. This means we must hold on to our beliefs and pursue a lifestyle and follow ambitions which agree with that.

There will be all kinds of pressures which will seek to make us deviate from this. These may come from others within our churches, but more likely they will come from the world outside. We cannot take it for granted that the whole of our life henceforth will be without conflict. The main thing is to be prepared for this and to seek God's help to keep us on the right path. We are also to live our lives daily in the light of all this.

Am I living in the light of what God has taught me?

Chapter 26
TWO KINDS OF FUTURE
(3:17-21)

What does the future hold for us? For the most part, the answer is that we do not know. As Christians we place today in God's hands and also leave the future with him. He knows what is best.

Like Paul, we have to live in the present, but thoughts of the future can affect the way in which we behave now. Paul offers himself as an example for others to follow. He also encourages his hearers to follow the lives of other faithful Christians around them.

There are three sections in this study, and each of these compares two ways of looking at life – a wrong way and a right way.

(1)   Concerning Morality

It is not just a matter of what we believe, but also of how we behave. There are so many people who live as enemies of the cross of Christ. It is possible to claim to be Christians, and yet to live in a way that belies this. People whose lives are like this may think they have got things right in the present, whereas, in way they do not understand, their destiny is destruction.

Paul speaks particularly of two wrongs. Firstly their god is their stomach. We all have physical needs, and it is right to trust God to provide what we need. But for some people this takes first place. They want to eat well, to enjoy lots of earthly comforts, to have an active sex life. The satisfaction of bodily needs is more important to them than that of their spiritual needs. This is understandable if a person does not make any claim to belong to God; but if a Christian embraces this attitude to life, something is seriously wrong.

Secondly, they glory in their shame. Attitudes to life, and particularly to sex, have altered over the years. People began to talk of the 'new morality' and 'situation ethics'. In other words, instead of adhering to clear biblical standards, it was felt that circumstances could sometimes justify deviant behaviour. One writer, who claimed to be writing from a Christian standpoint, even suggested that adultery could be a good thing if it helped a person to mature. In the early days of my ministry couples who came to me to prepare for marriage normally belonged to different addresses. In our own day, however, it is more usual for a couple to be already living together, with all that this implies.

Paul's life, however, was very different. He here says: "Join together in following my example, brothers and sisters, and just as you have us as a model, keep your eyes on those who live as we do." Paul was not the sort of man to teach one thing and do another. He made sure that his behaviour in no way belied his teaching. For the sake of the Lord's work, he never married, but he was in no way imposing this kind of celibacy on his hearers. If we are to teach others about observing good sexual standards, we must take care to follow those standards ourselves, otherwise we are simply using empty words. In 1 Corinthians 11:1 Paul says: "Follow my example, as I follow the example of Christ". The supreme example, therefore, is that of Christ himself.

(2) Concerning Worldliness

Paul says here, "their mind is set on earthly things". J. B. Phillips translates, "this world is the limit of their horizon". In other words, their thinking is limited to all that is of this world, and there is no room for spiritual thinking. The mind is very important, for it affects the way we behave. All our behaviour, whether good or evil, originates in the mind. It is as God renews the mind that we gain the ability to stand up against the world's pressures and dare to think in a Christian way.

The world tries hard to influence our thinking. It is possible to be doing a spiritual job and yet to be thinking of how to get more money, how to gain a higher position and so on, anything, in fact, which is for our own benefit. We may claim to regard the Cross as central in our lives yet live as enemies of the Cross. In our poor standards of morality and our longing for the things of this world, we reveal which side we are really on.

I accepted Jesus as Saviour when I was doing military service. At that time I was sleeping in a billet with many other airmen who were not Christians. I saw myself as a marked man for some of them were eager to see if I lived out what I professed. We all have that responsibility, whatever our circumstances.

As I have gone through the rest of my life, there have been times when I have fallen; but it has been important to recognize that this was not my real spiritual self but a reversion to my fallen nature. If we do fail at times, that is not who we really are. It is important to confess our sin and get back into God's presence as soon as we can.

Paul reminds the Philippians here that they are 'citizens of heaven'. At that time Philippi was a colony of Rome. It was like a little piece of the Roman Empire. Similarly, Christians are citizens of heaven. We may live alongside other people, but we belong to a different place. Wherever a Christian goes, there should be a little piece of heaven. How evident is this from our own lives? This world is not our permanent dwelling place. We look forward to going to heaven, where we really belong.

At the time of writing this I had a friend whose home in Florida was under threat from a malicious hurricane. Inside our home, with its bricks and mortar, we may feel safe; but if even this is not secure when the worst of the weather comes, what about our own lives when we face judgment? It is only by trusting in Christ that we can be secure and move on to somewhere better.

Paul says in 2 Corinthians 4:17-18: "For our light and momentary troubles are achieving for us an eternal glory that far outweighs them all. So we fix our eyes not on what is seen, but on what is unseen, since what is seen is temporary, but what is unseen is eternal."

(3) Concerning the Future

There are nominal Christians and true Christians. The former may be very familiar with spiritual things, yet remain uncommitted to God in a real and meaningful way. On the day of judgment he will hear the fearful words, "Depart from me; I never knew you".

The true Christian, however, is eagerly awaiting the return of Christ. Some of us have bodies that are fit and strong; others have bodies that are wearing out. On that day, however, he will transform our bodies, whatever their condition, so that they may be like his glorious body. This transformation is described in 1 Corinthians 15:43-4: "The body that is sown is perishable, it is raised imperishable; it is sown in dishonour, it is raised in glory; it is sown in weakness, it is raised in power; it is sown a natural body, it is raised a spiritual body".

All this is accomplished, we are told, through the power of Christ.

How do we feel about the future?

Chapter 27
QUESTIONS OF RELATIONSHIPS
(4:1-3)

We come now to the final chapter of this letter, which is full of encouragements. It is all about relationships. Paul makes various appeals to the Philippians in the hope that this will stir them to live out their faith properly in their relations with each other.

(1)   Paul's Relationship with the Philippians

There are three features here in the first verse which mark Paul's relationship with the Christians at Philippi.

First we see his love for them. In verse 1 he calls them 'my brothers and sisters, you whom I love and long for'. We are reminded of 1:7 where he told them "I have you in my heart".

This is no formal ministry: Paul writes to these Christians because he really cares for them. They are personal friends. We all experience love in many different forms; but there is a special Christian love which comes from God and unites us with one another. If in our church there is stress on doctrinal accuracy but no deep feeling for one another, then something vital is missing. In the Bible time and time again 'love' is described as the major Christian virtue.

Secondly we see his joy in them. He says: 'my joy and my crown'. When he sees how they are following the Lord, this gives him joy. In 1:4-5 he already described how he prayed for them with joy. What about the crown? This would be given to a winner in an athletics contest. When Paul has finished his work on earth, God will show his delight in those converted through his ministry by, in a sense, bestowing a crown upon him; though Paul's main aim is not simply that of getting his own reward! He has already said in 2:16: "And then I will be able to boast in the day of Christ that I did not run or labour in vain". Even so, it is not that Paul has earned this by his own striving: it is still a sign that God has been working in and through him all the time.

Thirdly we see his exhortation to them. He tells them to 'stand firm in the Lord in this way'. He does not take their future loyalty for granted. There will be opposition to face and there may be wrong man-made policies. For instance, the Judaizers will try to force the Law on to Gentile converts. They must continue to remember that it is their relationship with the Lord that matters most rather than a few outward observances. If they are truly following the Lord, then God will show them what is right and what is wrong as well as giving them the ability to stand firm.

(2) Their Relationship with One Another

Paul has already in Chapter 2 spoken of the importance of unity. Now he mentions a glaring example of disunity. There are two women, Eudodia and Syntyche, who do not get on with one another. If we are in disagreement with someone, we may think it is just a matter between the two of us, but it can also affect the wider fellowship. It is important, therefore, that these two women settle their differences as quickly as possible.

It is not as if they are merely fringe Christians. Both are important members of the local Christian community. Because of them, there is danger of the whole fellowship being riven in two. It is sad that Paul feels he has to mention them by name as a part of his letter.

If we are at loggerheads with someone else in our local church, we must take a look at our motivation. Is it just a personality clash, or is it a disagreement on some major doctrine? If the latter, then we must both examine our beliefs in the light of what Paul preaches. As contenders for the Gospel we must agree together on all important points. Naturally, we have personality differences as well as personal preferences, but these are matters we ought to be able to handle.

We have one advantage over these two women: we have the Bible. Through this, we have access to proper Christian truths. If our beliefs contradict what the Bible says, then we must be careful to put things right. In all honesty, there are some passages which may be interpreted in more than one way, and we then need the Spirit's guidance that we may come to a proper understanding.

There may be some passages on which we take different viewpoints, but not in such a way as to promote division. In such a case, we should have love and understanding for one another even though we may not have complete agreement.

If, however, we are making the same mistake as these women, it is important to examine our differences and come to an agreement as quickly as possible so that the progress of the Gospel is not hindered.

Not all denominations have the same emphases. In some it is the liturgy of worship which is regarded as really important; in some it is the quality of the worship songs; in others it is spiritual gifts, of which tongues has the pre-eminence; in others it is expository preaching that makes the Word come alive, and in others it is social contact which is thought to be vital. These must not be seen as rival factions. A church that is truly alive can embrace all of these at the same time. So it is not a matter of contention, but rather one of cooperation.

This does not mean that all Christians agree with each other exactly concerning their beliefs. There are major points of doctrine which must never be watered down; but there are also other less important issues where Christians do not all see in the same way. In such cases, it is not a matter of trying to get everyone to see things from our point of view, but rather of agreeing together on what is essential and allowing room for different ways of looking at things when nothing major is compromised.

These two women, then, are allowed to differ on some issues as long as they are still fully agreed on the essential truths of the Gospel.

Do you have any poor relationships with others that need to be put right?

112

Chapter 28
THE MOST IMPORTANT RELATIONSHIP
(4:4-7)

Our most important relationship is that which we have with the Lord. All other relationships derive from and depend on this one.

I remember a hospital patient whom I met during the early part of my ministry. He was a Baptist who was suffering from leukemia. His courage and his faith under such an affliction were a great encouragement to me. On one of my visits I asked him which passage of scripture he would like to read, and he chose these verses. The knowledge that the Lord was with him gave him such a comfort at that time. Shortly after that, he died.

There are five lessons contained in these precious verses.

(1)   A Lesson about Joy

There are some people who are more joyful than others. Whatever their circumstances, they still have a deep joy within.

This should be particularly true of us as Christians. We rely not on our outward circumstances, but on our relationship with Jesus Christ. He is the one who gives us joy. We take our joy from the knowledge that we belong to God, that he has saved us, and that he is working out his purpose in our lives. In some parts of the world Christians have to suffer terribly. Yet, as we read about them, we learn that even when their circumstances are so dire, they may still have joy. By contrast we have much more comfortable lives. But do we have this measure of joy? We are to be joyful not just when we are having a good day, but all the time.

(2)   A Lesson about Forbearance

How do we get on with others? Is there friction between us, or do we get on well with each other? If we look at different translations, the word used here may be 'forbearance' or 'gentleness'. In yet other translations it may be 'fair mindedness' or 'graciousness'. Simply because we are human beings, we have our own failings. So do others. These failings may easily cause friction in our relationships. However, the more we become aware of our own failings, the more we are able to make allowances for the failings of others. We are all in equal need of God's help in improving our character and our behaviour.

(3)   A Lesson about our Lord's Coming

In New Testament days, people were expecting Jesus to come back at any time. Thus they lived their lives in the light of all this. It helped them to deal with their troubles, for they knew that these were only temporary. It also helped them to make good choices concerning their behaviour. Who would want to be in the middle of doing something wrong at the time of Jesus' return? Many centuries have passed since then, and we have lost our sense of immediacy. And yet we too should be living so as to be ready for the return of Christ at any time.

(4)   A Lesson about Prayer

Prayer means talking to God and listening to him. We may not actually see him, but we can still talk with him. This is the best antidote to anxiety. So we are told here: "Do not be anxious about anything, but in every situation, by prayer and petition, with thanksgiving, present your requests to God."

Life does not always go smoothly. It is easy to find things to worry about. That is where prayer comes in. Prayer means sharing these problems with God. It is a way of casting our burdens upon him so that we do not have to carry them ourselves.

Prayer can take various forms. Here Paul uses four words to describe it. The first is a general word, two other terms speak of making specific requests to God, and the other word reminds us of the importance of thanking God when our prayers have been answered. We know that our prayers are not a mere flight of fancy, but God hears our prayers and will make an appropriate answer. It is good to know that we are not alone, but enjoy his sustenance and his help.

(5) A Lesson about Peace

One result of prayer is that God brings us into a state of peace. A person may walk into a hospital ward and say to a patient, "Don't worry"; but it is the patient who has to deal with the condition, not the speaker. When we confide our problems to the Lord, however, he takes our burdens upon himself and so gives us peace of heart.

It is important, then, that we share our burdens with the Lord. He may remove the problems entirely or he may just give us peace to deal with them. Paul says here: "And the peace of God, which transcends all understanding, will guard your hearts and your minds in Christ Jesus." It is not a peace which is given to everybody: it is given to those who share their problems with the Lord.

Now it is no longer merely a problem of trying to find some inner strength, but of leaning on the Lord, who is fully able to deal with our situation. He will ensure that the problems, whatever they are, do not take us away from him, but enable us to lean on him more confidently. There is no room for unbelief and despair when we are confident that he is in control of those things which we do not understand.

Have you learned to share your worries with God so that you don't have to bear them yourself?

Chapter 29
FOOD FOR THE MIND
(4:8,9)

In some versions this section begins with the words 'finally' or 'in conclusion'. It might be better to use the words 'and so' for in this section there is a close link with what has just preceded it. Paul has spoken about peace of mind: if we want to preserve this, then we must be careful as to how we feed our minds.

We must take care about what we read. Sometimes when a man is arrested on charges of violence and rape he is found to possess books which advocate such behaviour. In this age, however, his reading is more likely to come from something on the internet. Material found on doubtful websites may encourage the user to put these suggestions into practice. Films too may have an adverse effect: after the release of the film, "A Clockwork Orange", many years ago, there was an outbreak of group rape. Even the ungodly talk that stems from unwise friendships may lead us to take wrongful actions. How important, then, it is to expose our mind to the right subjects.

A little further down, Paul uses the words: "think about such things". What things? Things that are excellent or praiseworthy. This is good in principle, but what things in particular is he thinking of? In verse 8 six words are used to describe our thoughts. Let us take a close look at them.

(1)   Things that are true

This is not so easy to do. There are things which appear reliable but which will not stand up to scrutiny. We have recently heard of high rise flats built apparently with great respect for their safety; but subsequent effects have demonstrated that all was not as it seemed.

There are programmes on television which suggest that sexual irregularity may in the right circumstances be a good thing, and this is reflected in the high incidence of partnerships rather than marriage and the frequency of divorce. If our minds are focused on the great truths we read about in Scripture and on God himself, then we can be a good witness to others.

(2)   Things that are noble

The word translated 'noble' could also be translated as 'honourable', 'reverend' or 'worthy'. We are to think of things which have the dignity of holiness about them. We may go to visit a beautiful cathedral, and, in admiring its features, find that we are also impressed with noble feelings. Historically, the Puritans were serious and dignified, but they might easily be called 'killjoys'. A Christian takes his faith seriously, but this leads to positive, well controlled behaviour which reflects the God he serves, a way of life which brings others nearer to God.

(3)   Things that are right

Many people prefer to do things which give them pleasure. But the word used here speaks of doing our duty to God and to men. If we put God first, others next and self last then we may get some idea of what is required here. Things are 'right' when they are inspired by God, conform to his character and are used in his service. They are right when they do not stand in conflict with anything we read about in the scriptures.

It is good when we are so in touch with God that we naturally think of what is right and put it into practice.

(4)   Things that are pure

In our society there is a lot of moral freedom and that freedom easily becomes 'license'. Everything is permissible if it feels good. In Titus 1:15 we read "To the pure, all things are pure".

This verse, if misunderstood, could lead us into danger. If our hearts were morally pure in every respect, we would have clear moral insight into every situation; but the problem is that we are not so mature and are easily tainted. We should therefore avoid all that would damage us morally and pay attention to all that brings us closer to our holy God.

(5)   Things that are lovely

We may use the word 'lovely' too loosely. Literally this expression means 'things which call forth love'. I can deal with others in different ways. I can be rough in my dealings with them and stir up bitterness and fear, or I can seek to build up a reciprocal love. It is a matter of how concerned I am for others as people.

(6)   Things that are honourable

This is not an easy word to translate. Sometimes it is translated 'of good report'. Moffat has 'high toned'. Literally it means 'things that are suitable for God to hear'. Do the things I say meet with his approval? Sometimes we may have special visitors to our home who arrive unexpectedly, just when the place is at its untidiest. The way to avoid this problem is to keep it tidy all the time. God is not just on an occasional visit, he is there at all times. How important, then, that we keep our thoughts clean and wholesome.

Here Paul is not just producing a few ideas, he is talking about a whole way of life. It is not theory, but is taken from his own way of behaving. He says: "Whatever you have learned or received or heard from me, or seen in me – put it into practice." Paul is not just giving them some objective teaching : he himself serves as an example for others to follow.

Here is a lesson too for us to be careful about our own behaviour. It is no use speaking to others about our faith if our actions belie what we say. It is as we live out the Christian faith in practice that we can be an encouragement to others.

Of course, the greatest example to follow is that of Jesus himself; but if we are true followers of his, we will reflect his character in the way we behave.

If this is true of us, then the God of peace will be with us.

He is a God who wants to bring peace, not discord.

How many of these qualities do we display in our own lives?

Chapter 30
THE SECRET OF CONTENTMENT
(4:10-13)

Only as this letter draws to a close do we learn the special circumstances which prompted Paul to write it. We have already learned that Paul was in prison and that he was sending Epaphroditus back to Philippi. Only now, however, do we learn that the Philippian Christians have shown their concern for Paul by sending him money.

Why did they not send money before? There is no rebuke concerning this: although they really cared for Paul they did not have opportunity to show it. But now they have shown the extent of their concern through a gift of money, and this makes Paul feel happy.

Not that he only feels happy when he is in receipt of gifts, for he has learned to be content in each and every situation. He is also happy here not just because of their gifts but because of the loving concern that lies behind them.

This brings us to the two main lessons which we observe in this passage.

(1) Be Satisfied with What you Have

Let us repeat Paul's words in v.11: "I have learned to be content whatever the circumstances". For Paul it was not just a matter of being short of money: he was short of freedom as well. Some people would have complained about this, but for Paul that was not an option.

Many years ago I was with a group of fellow curates at a post ordination training conference. The canon who was in charge told us that money was the root of evil; but I did not agree. It is the love of money that is the root of evil: money itself is neutral, as are our other possessions. This is clearly stated in 1 Timothy 6:10 and elaborated in verses 17 to 19.

For Paul it was not just a matter of telling others to behave in a certain way, but of setting a good example himself. So he says in verse 12: "I know what it is to be in need, and I know what it is to have plenty. I have learned the secret of being content in every and any situation, whether well fed or hungry, whether living in plenty or in want".

There are dangers belonging to both conditions. If we are short of money we may envy those who have more, and that denotes a spirit of covetousness. If we have plenty of money we may grow proud of it and neglect those who have too little, and so portray a spirit of pride.

It is interesting to see how much Jesus speaks about money in the Gospels. This is a topic which affects all of us and our attitude to it reveals the genuineness or otherwise of our faith.

The inequality between rich and poor may raise many questions. There is an old hymn which reads:

"The rich man in his castle,

The poor man at his gate,

God made them high and lowly

And ordered their estate."

Some people refuse to sing this verse, and, indeed, it has been excluded from some of our hymn books. Yes, in a sense, God did make both the rich and the poor man, but that does not mean that he has no concern for the poor nor that the rich man should not feel obliged to do something about this inequality.

Of course, our primary responsibility as Christians is to share the Gospel with others so that they may come to experience God's salvation for themselves. But if we have a true heart for others, will it not also include a concern for their practical problems? Can we be content as Westerners to enjoy our comfortable lifestyle whilst ignoring the plight of those who struggle for survival?

Over the past few years, as the number of problems for Christians has grown – from disastrous weather conditions to severe persecution

– so has the number of Christian groups which do all they can to bring relief to those in distress. Although we, as Christians, are chiefly concerned to bring others to the knowledge of Christ, we cannot ignore such practical needs, and more and more of us are showing such concern through our giving.

Compared with such needy people, we have comfortable lives. Yet there are so many people who are driven by the ambition to procure more wealth and power. It is true that there are many Christians who acquire this by legitimate means and for good reasons, but this also faces them with the challenge as to how best they should use their wealth. It depends whether our confidence is chiefly in God or in the material world.

(2) Strength for this Comes from Christ.

How then can we be satisfied whatever our condition? Paul explains this in verse 13 with the words "I can do all this through him who gives me strength." It is not a human achievement, but is divinely inspired.

A stoic, William Ernest Henley, who was also a poet, once wrote:

"It matters not how strait the gate,

How charged with punishments the scroll,

I am the master of my fate,

I am the captain of my soul."

We may, in a sense, admire such an attitude, but it comes through human fortitude and not through God's empowering.

The humanist believes he can achieve anything if he just tries hard enough; but history does not bear this out. It is full of stories about human failure. Conscious of our weaknesses, it is as we come to God for strength that we are able to achieve anything.

Just see how God has changed people in the past. John Newton in his seafaring days told such juicy stories that even his hardened companions were appalled; yet he became a gracious and loving pastor. Gladys Aylward was a simple parlour maid, but when she observed God's call to go to China she was able to learn a difficult language and deal with all kinds of emergencies. A rector in North Belfast during the 'troubles', when all the rectory windows were blown out by a bomb, had the courage to continue ministering to others in that dangerous area. We can do all things through Christ, who strengthens us.

We may not always understand why God puts us into difficult circumstances, but he is well able to deal with these.

In the year 1648 a man called Jeremiah Burroughs brought out a book called "The Rare Jewel of Christian Contentment". In this book he wrote: "Contentment is the inward, quiet, gracious frame of spirit, freely submitting to and taking pleasure in God's disposal in every condition".

Do you have problems in your life that you need to bring to God?

Chapter 31
CHRISTIAN GIVING
(4:14-20)

The Church cannot function without money. Yet it is only too easy to give the impression that money raising is the chief activity that we embrace. If we are functioning properly as a local church, the provision of money for our needs should occur readily as an expression of God's work within us.

Although Paul is writing here about Christian giving, he does not embrace topics that are of current concern such as stewardship and tithing. He is still writing about how the Philippian Christians have helped him personally with finance.

However, we can deduce from this three principles which are important for us today.

(1) Giving Deepens Fellowship

Paul shows his gratitude for what they had done in the past. According to verse 15, when they were new Christians and Paul was setting out from Macedonia on his missionary work, the only church that shared with him in the matter of giving and receiving was this one. They particularly helped him when he was ministering in Thessalonica. When he writes of 'giving and receiving' he probably means that those who give financially are likely to receive spiritual blessings.

But Paul was not uniform in his attitude to this topic. Earlier he had refused to take money from the Thessalonians and from the Corinthians, lest this should be used as a criticism against him. He thus judged each case on its own merits. His main aim was not to raise money but to preach the gospel effectively.

With the Philippians, however, there was no problem: he was happy to receive such help and he thanked them for it.

Each time he was in particular need, it was their gifts which helped him out.

Giving, then, is not just an external thing: it is a practical demonstration of the meaning of Christian fellowship. Because we love others, we are happy to share with them. It is a blessing to those who give and to those who receive.

(2)   Giving is a Good Investment

In verse 17 Paul writes: "Not that I desire your gifts, what I desire is that more be credited to your account". In verse 19 he goes on to say "And my God will meet all your needs according to the riches of his glory in Christ Jesus." They had given because of a genuine concern for Paul's welfare; but in a sense they are also recipients, for they become all the more aware of God's blessing on their lives.

It is regarded as a good investment when our money is in an account that is favoured with good interest. How much better this is than simply putting money to one side to be taken and used as and when needed. These Philippians did not put their money into a bank account: they gave it to Paul for his needs. In doing so, however, they had built up a lot of credit in the spiritual account which they had with God. So it is not so much a matter of trying to get more money but of using our money in such a way that we gain such spiritual credit with God. Though, of course, that is not our main motive!

We are reminded of Jesus' words in Matthew 6:19-20: "Do not store up for yourselves treasures on earth, where moths and vermin destroy, and where thieves break in and steal. But store up for yourselves treasures in heaven, where moths and vermin do not destroy, and where thieves do not break in and steal". However rich we are materially, we cannot take any of our money to heaven when we die; but if we have used our money and other gifts to bring spiritual good, then we have a lot of credit attached to our name when it is time for heaven.

But Paul goes on to say that God is able to meet their every need. It seems that they did not give out of their wealth, but out of their limited resources. Paul therefore wanted to reassure them that, if their funds were low because of their generosity, God was well able to fulfill their needs. I find that in my last few years I have more funds available than at any time in my life; yet I can look back to times when I gave out of my limited resources and found that, like the Philippians, I always had enough for my needs.

(3)   Giving is Pleasing to God

See how Paul in verse 18 describes the gifts which the Philippians have given him through Epathroditus: "They are a fragrant offering, an acceptable sacrifice, pleasing to God".

In the past the word 'sacrifice' referred mainly to the killing of animals and offering them to God in the Temple. When Jesus sacrificed himself for us on the Cross, all this changed. It was no longer necessary to slaughter animals: what God required was that we should respond to what Jesus had done for us by the sacrifice of our hearts to him, and this would lead us to be generous in our personal giving. This was now the sort of sacrifice that was pleasing to God. It was an ongoing feature.

It is not just a matter of monetary offerings. We read in Hebrews 13:13: "Through Jesus, therefore, let us continually offer to God a sacrifice of praise - the fruit of lips that openly profess his name".   So it is not just our external offerings that are acceptable to God but the quality of our praise and worship.

Going back to the main subject here, however, the giving of money for God's work is not seen merely as a monetary transaction: it is also seen as an act of worship, which honours God. Some people may consider that going round with a plate for offerings in a service of worship is an intrusion; but here we learn that this itself is to be seen as an act of worship. We should not just give on the spur of the moment but pray beforehand about how much we should give.

Our giving also should be extended to include all manner of situations where people are in need. We as Christians have a responsibility to share our money with others, especially those who are in very troubled circumstances. However, it is good to ensure that any organisation which claims to help the needy is reliable and is doing a good job. There are some who would take advantage of such situations to delude others. That is why I like to know all about a charity to which I am invited to contribute money before I actually do so.

The attitude with which we give money is also important. Do we give cheerfully? Do we give prayerfully? Do we give freely? Do we give generously? As we read in 2 Corinthians 9:7: "Each of you should give what you have decided in your heart to give, not reluctantly or under compulsion, for God loves a cheerful giver".

If giving is seen as an act of worship, then it is perfectly fitting that Paul ends this section with a doxology in verse 20:

"To our God and Father be glory for ever and ever. Amen."

Take a look at your own giving and ask yourself whether you think it honours God.

Chapter 32
FINAL GREETINGS
(4:21-23)

There are various ways in which we can finish a letter. Often we simply write "Yours sincerely". If it is a Christian writing to a Christian we may write "Yours in Christ".

Paul, however, writes rather more than that. He sends greetings not just from himself but from other Christians, and he manages to make three extra references to God just in this brief space.

Two of these verses are about greetings and one is about grace. Let us see what we can learn from them as we bring the study of this book to a close.

(1)   Greetings

It is normal when we meet up with people to greet them. But it is also possible to greet people who live a long way from us. In our own day we can do this by e-mail, Messenger, 'What's App', or by some words on our smart-phone, and that is just for starters.... In Paul's day it could have involved a long journey before the greeting was passed on. How different from the early days of my missionary service, when the only contact with 'home' was a weekly letter. In this case the recipients are the Christians in Philippi.

Here Paul invites the Christians there who read his letter to pass his greetings on to others around them who will remember him. In some translations they are addressed as saints. In modern parlance this might lead us to think of people with a halo over their heads or who always act in a particularly holy way. But the term refers not so much to their actions as to their relationship with God. They are God's holy people, and that is what marks them out from others. If we are Christians, then we can claim the same relationship. Of course, this should affect the way we behave, but that is not the initial meaning of the term. We are the ones who are privileged to know that we belong to God. We are his holy people. Are we conscious of belonging to God in this special way? If so, this should have a profound effect on how we live.

Although it is Paul who is sending his greetings to them, he simply considers himself as part of the local Christian community. All Christians brothers and sisters in his locality join with Paul in sending greetings. It should encourage the Christians at Philippi to know that they have Christian brothers and sisters who live a long way from their own homes, but who are still concerned for them. He continues this theme by calling them "all God's people here". Sometimes as Christians we may feel rather isolated. It is good therefore to recall that God has his own people in many other parts of the world.

Sometimes God's people may be found in unexpected places. Here they include members of Caesar's household. Caesar himself would not claim to be a Christian, yet among his servants are people who do make that claim. In our own world there are places like North Korea, Somalia, Eritrea and many other countries where it is difficult and dangerous to be a Christian; yet God still has his representatives in such places. Let us take encouragement from this and also bear these people up in our prayers.

(2) Grace

In the final verse of this letter, Paul talks about grace. He says: "The grace of the Lord Jesus Christ be with your Spirit. Amen."

The word 'grace' here indicates that God is good to us when we do not deserve it. Another translation would be 'unmerited favour'. It is not as if we have worked hard to stir up good conduct marks. God accepts us with all our sins and weaknesses, and that is simply because we have come to belong to Jesus Christ. Sometimes, when we have gone astray, it is only too easy to feel that we are far from God; but if we are 'in Christ', we are close to him, whether we feel it or not, and this recollection should assure us of an ongoing relationship with him. Often in my walks I find myself talking to God, and usually in my heart there is a mixture of grief and confidence.

Paul had formerly been a keen Jew, but an enemy to the newly formed Christian Church, as he regarded its teaching as heresy. Only after Christ met with him on the Damascus road did all this change. It was not that Paul (or Saul as he was then) had had time to think things through, but God's grace came upon him dramatically and completely changed his approach.

Each of the Philippian Christians has his own personal story. Their conversion may not have been as dramatic as Paul's, but the result is the same. They have been changed by grace. In the same way, we must not rely on being brought up in church, having Christian parents, reading the Bible often and so on. Christ has to do a new work within us. We too are saved by grace and not by personal striving; and we are in need of that continuing grace in order that we may grow in our Christian life.

So the prayer that grace may be upon us is not empty words, but a demonstration that we need the Lord in each and every situation.

Grace was present in the opening greeting, and it is appropriate that Paul ends by speaking of grace again. In fact the whole life of each Philippian Christian, as well as that of Christians around the world today, is entirely dependent on God's grace. Without this we would not have assurance of God's acceptance and the strength to live out our Christian lives properly.

What evidence is there in my own life that I am not depending on my own resources but on living by the grace of God?

Printed in Poland
by Amazon Fulfillment
Poland Sp. z o.o., Wrocław